Fugitive Information

Internal Affairs
Prayers to the Moon
Women Respond to the Men's Movement (editor)

Fugitive Information

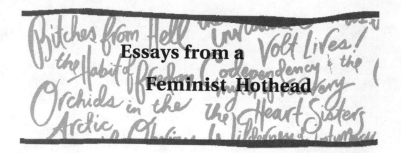

Essays from a
Feminist Hothead

Kay Leigh Hagan

Pandora
An Imprint of HarperSanFrancisco*Publishers*

FIRST EDITION

Library of Congress Cataloging-in-Publication Data
Hagan, Kay Leigh.
    Fugitive information: essays from a feminist hothead / Kay Leigh Hagan.
      p. cm.
    Includes bibliographical references.
    ISBN 0-06-250660-9 (acid-free paper)
    1. Feminism   2. Patriarchy.   I. Title.
    HQ1150.H34 1993
    305.42—dc20   92-56421
                                                            CIP

ISBN 0-06-250660-9
93 94 95 96 97 RRD(H) ❖ 10 9 8 7 6 5 4 3 2 1
This edition is printed on acid-free paper that meets the American National
Standards Institute Z39.48 Standard.

Contents

Fugitive Information:

Feminism on the Run

ugitive information is a term taken from computer jargon, referring to data that escapes from the system. Refusing to respond to a programmer's commands, it appears on the screen of its own will, in its own time, then disappears without a trace. Fugitive information is, literally, out of control. In other realms, fugitives fleeing from danger seek out safety and allies. Pursuing a feminist vision over the past two decades, I have often felt like a fugitive—stealthily navigating through the daily maze of domination, seeking a sanctuary of connection and community, creating culture on the run.

Feminism does have its dangers. According to the temperament of the times, espousing such views can get you jailed, exiled, assassinated, ridiculed, censored, reviled, or burned alive.[1] I find it difficult to grasp, and not a little absurd, that advocating a simple matter of human rights—that women are entitled to equal pay, equal opportunity, equal protection under the law, control over our bodies, and safety from male violence—continues to raise such a ruckus among reasonable people. Of course, it might be pointed out that one needn't be a feminist to provoke such treatment—being a woman is enough.

Writing about feminism carries its own particular dangers. Attempts to define, describe, or in any way limit feminist ideas to the page risk depriving this lively body of thought of what I consider its essential nature. To me, feminism is at its best on the run, in motion. Its ideas become real in the daily lives of women inventing freedom as we go. Feminism is created constantly by women questioning everything, from a society that deems us inferior to men, and all its laws—written and unwritten—customs, images, institutions, and socially sanctioned attitudes, to the feminist movement itself. Challenge, debate, and process make up the critical consciousness feminism encourages us to develop, and the movement is hardly exempt from its own scrutiny. I have been exhilarated and alarmed at once by the vigor with which advocates of feminism challenge one another as we attempt to turn theory into action. To walk what you talk is fundamental to a feminist view, and when we encounter in each other evidence of racism, ableism, classism, homophobia, and other legacies of our conditioning under dominance, judgment can be swift.

As a writer, then, I have approached feminism with more than a little caution because I know that a moving thing cannot be truly apprehended when confined to the page. This healthy respect led me to follow a rather circuitous route to the ultimate destination of this book. The essays began as singular questions in my own mind as I read my first feminist books, then grew into conversations with hundreds of women who, like me, were searching for ways to apply feminist theory to our daily choices. Since feminism is a collaborative effort, it seemed appropriate to open my writing process to the community for whom I write.

So, as individual pamphlets, these essays were circulated in draft over the course of three years to a subscriber network that was asked, How do these ideas relate to your life? A newsletter publishing the responses was circulated to link subscribers with one another, and the essays were finally revised in dialogue with that community of readers, completing the circle. Portions of the critiques and responses from subscribers are included here after each essay, to share their insights and to put the evolution of the work in proper context. A subscriber writes:

> *I like the name "fugitive information" because it sounds rebellious and because I feel like a fugitive in this world, given my beliefs and thoughts. But also I see a fugitive mentality as something very positive for women if it is developed self-consciously: like the underground railroad or the sanctuary movement or the Jane Collective in Chicago, which clandestinely provided safe abortions to women pre-Roe v. Wade. If we can't "recover" from oppression, we can strategize and organize to change things, and if we take seriously the need for this government to keep women "in their places," and if we study the history of the government's counterintelligence activities against all movements for progressive change, we could start to believe that at times, it's a good thing to be a fugitive.*

When I launched the *Fugitive Information* essay series in 1989, I challenged myself to write about questions that scared me, ideas about which I was uncertain, and controversial subjects that intimidated me. My intention was not so much to find answers but to articulate the questions more precisely. While the subjects of the essays are varied—from codependency to the erasure of women's heritage to the dilemma of heterosexual feminism to the outrage of male violence against women to the celebration of women loving women over time—the theme of the collection is internalized oppression: How are we taught to collude with our own oppression?

Fortunately my somewhat morbid fascination with this discouraging phenomenon chronicled in these essays has helped me discover its probable antidote—what Gloria Steinem calls the revolution from within. The paradigm shift from dominator to partnership values so desperately needed in the world at large begins when we change our own minds, replacing an inheritance of obsession with control and self-hatred with a commitment to community and self-respect. The urgency and magnitude of our global crisis notwithstanding, I take heart daily in the words of Marilyn French: "No movement has ever been more than an accumulation of small motions of people acting within their own spheres. In rearranging our lives, we participate in rearranging the life of society."[2]

Because the theories that work best are the ones that offer practical guidance, some of the essays are followed by a list of suggestions to help move from theory to practice. A resource section at the end of the book, organized by essay, lists related books and films for readers with hungry minds. And for those who feel a need to connect or a desire for action, subscription

information for *Fugitive Information,* the continuing essay series and newsletter, is included in the Afterword.

Although I bear ultimate responsibility for authoring these essays, the collection contains a flow of ideas from many women—
and a few men—with whom I have found refuge. Because we
continue to discuss, argue, pontificate, scrutinize, and evolve our
ideas, this book might best be viewed as a restless pool where the
river water pauses to swell for a moment before continuing its
journey toward the ocean. There, I trust, it will make its contribution to the mighty rising of feminism's Third Wave.

NOTES

1   See the lives of Emma Goldman, Voltairine de Cleyre, Andrea
Dworkin, Joan of Arc, Pauline Bart, Anita Hill, Hillary Clinton, the countless women murdered during the witch burnings, et al.

2   Marilyn French, *Beyond Power: On Women, Men, and Morals*
(New York: Simon & Schuster, 1985), 545.

Volt Lives! Diary of a Hothead

We need to know how patriarchy works.
We need to know how women disappear,
why we are initiated into a culture
where women have no visible past,
and what will happen if we make that past visible and real.
If the process is not to be repeated again,
if we are to transmit to the next generation of women
what was denied transmission to us, we need to know
how to break the closed circle of male power which permits
men to go on producing knowledge about themselves,
pretending that we do not exist.

Dale Spender[1]

I did not intend to fall in love with a woman who lived a hundred years ago. But when I picked out a postcard photograph of Voltairine de Cleyre from my collection of "strong women" images several years ago and pinned it to the bulletin board in front of my desk, something moved inside me. How can I describe her? Curly hair pulled back from her shining, solemn face, around her neck a black velvet ribbon holding a brooch in the fashion of 1891. Her eyes, enormous, the burning gaze of an angel of truth. In this photograph, taken when she was twenty-five, she is not smiling. She is a woman on a mission. Months later, when I finally thought to turn the card over to find out who she was, I learned why I found her image so compelling. Voltairine was a hothead.

> *Voltairine de Cleyre (1866-1912) American anarchist, freethinker, and feminist. Born in rural Michigan and educated in a Catholic convent, she converted to anarchism after the hanging of the Haymarket martyrs in 1887. Most of her adult life was spent in Philadelphia, where she was a founder of the Ladies' Liberal League and a teacher among the Jewish immigrant poor. An inspired speaker and writer, she published hundreds of poems, essays, and stories, mainly on themes of social rebellion. . . . Wounded by an assassin in 1902, she refused to press charges, returning good for evil in the spirit of Tolstoy. During her last years, she was arrested after a free-speech demonstration in Philadelphia, supported the Mexican Revolution, and taught at an anarchist school in Chicago, where she died in 1912. She was buried in the Waldheim Cemetery beside the graves of the Haymarket anarchists whose martyrdom had inspired her life. Emma Goldman called her the "poet-rebel, the liberty-loving artist, the greatest woman anarchist of America."[2]*

These brief biographical notes brought my college-educated ignorance into full view. Not only had I never heard of de Cleyre, I could claim only hazy impressions of anarchism, Tolstoy, and the Mexican Revolution. The Haymarket martyrs were a complete mystery to me, and my strongest memories of Emma Goldman came from Maureen Stapleton's depiction of her in the movie *Reds* and a quote from a popular button, "If I can't dance I don't want your revolution," which I'm probably misquoting at that. Voltairine's gaze reached one hundred years into the future and moved me from ignorance to curiosity. Suddenly I wanted to know her. This is powerful magic.

With the quiet obsession of the infatuated, I began to gather information about Voltairine and immediately discovered some similarities between us. Like her, I write, speak, and teach. Like her, I face the turn of the century at a time of great crisis. Like her, I feel driven to confront a social value system gone berserk. Like Voltairine, I am a hothead.

> *Let every woman ask herself:*
> *"Why am I the slave of Man? Why is my brain said*
> *not to be the equal of his brain? Why is my work not*
> *paid equally with his? Why must my body be con-*
> *trolled by my husband? Why may he take my labor*
> *in the household, giving me in exchange what he*
> *deems fit? Why may he take my children from me?*
> *Will them away while yet unborn?"*
> *Let every woman ask.*
>
> Voltairine de Cleyre, 1890[3]

In 1988 I carried Dale Spender's eight-hundred-page book, *Women of Ideas (and What Men Have Done to Them)*, to the International Feminist Book Fair in Montreal, for the sole purpose of asking her to sign it. Her book helped to fill the vast empty hallways I had discovered in my mind, that interior library which should have been a treasure trove of women's thoughts, writings, and achievements—my own cultural heritage. I wanted to meet the woman who had dared to pose and answer the question, How are women erased from history? Before reading Spender, I'd not been interested in women's history even though for over a decade I'd been an active and vocal feminist. Why the lack of interest? True confessions: Whenever I saw the words *women's history,* a voice inside immediately said, "BORING."

Will the elegant tactics of internalized oppression never cease to amaze me? The message encoded in that single word: Women don't do or say anything important, never have, never will, and if they do or did, it makes/made no difference anyway, so skip it. The result: In the privacy of my own mind, I elected to reject my heritage as a woman. Almost anything seemed more interesting to me, and, voracious reader though I am, I had self-selected a library virtually devoid of the work of my foresisters. While it is painfully true that millions of women have been dropped from the history books, rendered invisible, thus making it impossible for me to know of them, somehow I had been convinced that even if they did exist, they would be *boring.* This, too, is powerful magic.

So there I stood, unwitting prisoner of misogyny, my mind hermetically sealed against the enormous wealth of empowerment available from my elders. In my arrogant ignorance, I remember feeling desperately alone and demoralized as I strengthened my feminist beliefs, worked for women's rights, and reinvented the wheel. While it could have been one of many excellent books, for me it was Dale Spender's work that unlocked my personal prison door. Along with a brave and diligent generation of feminist scholars, she has recovered great portions of our precious heritage from patriarchy's landfill, making it possible to trace the brilliance of women through time.

Through short summaries of almost two hundred women of achievement, from Aphra Behn to Adrienne Rich, *Women of Ideas* tracks the ways men have managed to erase our predecessors, largely by discrediting them through personal attack and avoiding discussion of ideas.[4] Reading Spender, I was awestruck by my ignorance of the broad, complex, and profound accomplishments of women. The overwhelming proof that I was not the first and only filled me with a pride, strange and strong: I am one of an infinitely long line of women who recognize injustice and confront it, women who have a vision and live it, who remember through our cells another kind of world and believe in it. Power, so unfamiliar and fundamental it embarrasses me, surged in my heart. I felt inspired, optimistic, and confident. No wonder our heritage is denied us. There is a method to the madness of men.

Spender did not disappoint: Tall and bold and dressed entirely in purple, she held me spellbound with her Australian accent and searing wit as she addressed the audience of feminists from around the world. "I'm not so concerned about equality with men anymore," she declared, "I'm more interested in *remuneration*." She signed my dog-eared book with a purple pen. Another hothead.

> *I never expect men to give us liberty. No, women, we are not worth it, until we take it.*
>
> Voltairine de Cleyre, 1891

With the help of Celeste Tibbits, hothead librarian, I began to uncover information about Voltairine.[5] I learned she was named after the philosopher Voltaire by her father, who wanted a son, and she was known as a headstrong, emotional child of "evident intelligence." Having taught herself to read at the age of four, Volt (as I nicknamed her) would often sit alone with a book in her favorite tree. Her family was brutally poor, and her parents separated before she was twelve.

Like anyone in love, I looked for Voltairine everywhere. I was on a lecture tour that winter which took me to both coasts and through a good chunk of the Midwest. I first read her actual words in a collection of political essays in Boston's majestic city library. She explains in *The Making of an Anarchist* how in adolescence, her rebellion against a restrictive convent education encouraged her to become a "freethinker," a term that seems radically alien to our own media-infested minds. In *The Dominant Idea,* she describes her sense that a certain theme of values prevails in each historical era. In her case, at the turn of the last century, it was "the Much Making of Things . . . things ugly, things harmful, things useless, and at best largely unnecessary." I shuddered to imagine what Volt might think of the Hypermart? the Shopping channel? a Salad Shooter?

In Los Angeles, on a whim, I checked the card catalog in the rare-book section of the UCLA library. Jackpot! A small volume, privately published in letterpress, with a single essay written years after Voltairine's death—Emma Goldman's remembrance of her. In the ritual of procedures surrounding rare books, I was admitted to a special room with only a notebook—pencils were supplied and no ink pens allowed—supervised by a librarian on an elevated desk. At one point, I raised the fragile chapbook closer to my eyes, opening it too wide, and was startled by the supervisor's gentle reprimand "not to crack the spine." I felt a rush of reverence for my task and returned to my feverishly penciled notes, copying quotations and savoring the tactile connection with my increasingly beloved Voltairine.

> *How, then, should [we] know of the wonderful spirit that was born in some obscure town in the State of Michigan, and who lived in poverty all of her life, but who by sheer force of will pulled herself out of a living grave, cleared her mind from the darkness of superstition,—turned her face to the sun, perceived a great ideal and determinedly carried it to every corner of her native land?*
>
> Emma Goldman, on Voltairine de Cleyre

Outside Lansing, Michigan, I cruised onto the freeway and headed for the village of Leslie, Voltairine's birthplace. I didn't expect to find any real evidence of her—she was there for only a year or so as an infant—but the opportunity to visit her place of birth was irresistible. The land was rolling hills, gentle sloping farmland, bare and monochrome in the winter of mid-March. As the miles passed, I mused on the properties and characteristics of a hothead, "a woman in love," says artist Laurie Anderson.

What do I mean by hothead?

The mind ablaze. The hungry brain. Awareness. Epiphany. Insight. Outwitting the rape of the mind with vigilant attention to the mundane details of collusion. The vision of freedom, a beacon in the distance, growing closer with each step, guiding my direction with its steady glow. Fearless in the face of my own anger, empowered by that anger to outrage, my heart pounding with the desire to change, and changing—daring at last to love my self, to step into power, embrace my influence, and feel my vital connection to nature, community, and cosmos. Imagining the impossible, relishing the challenge. A hothead thinks big.

Leslie is still a small town, a simple crossroads, a few older buildings. I stopped in at city hall and talked to a clerk about my quest. She showed me some old plat maps, the grids drawn by hand and lettered in the feathery script of the last century. I scanned them quickly, searching for "de Cleyre" in hopes of finding at least the site of her family's home. No luck. I mailed a few cards with her photograph from the post office to get the Leslie postmark, said a blessing, and moved on.

> *Every individual should have a room or rooms for himself [sic] exclusively . . . a "closet" where each could "pray in secret" without some persons who love him assuming the right to walk in and do as they please. And do you know how I was pleased beyond measure the other day to find that William Godwin and Mary Wollstonecraft taught and as far as possible practiced the same thing, just 100 years ago.*
>
> *Voltairine de Cleyre, in a letter to her mother*

I gathered details about Voltairine with delight. I noted that she was finding inspiration from the past as I was, that she worked for a national day of recognition for writer and activist Mary Wollstonecraft, who preceded her by a hundred years. Volt wrote poetry, essays, short stories, and political treatises that were much admired. She lived a marginal existence, supporting herself by teaching the underprivileged, especially Russian Jews. She was tormented throughout her life by poor health, a relentless ringing in her ears, and chronic infections escalating after she survived an assassination attempt by a former student in

1902 (shot four times at point-blank range). She loved beauty in all things, inspired the same in others, and formed passionate partnerships throughout her life. When visiting England in 1897, she went to Stonehenge, saw Ibsen's *Doll's House* and Sarah Bernhardt playing Camille, and danced into the night. After her death, she was informally canonized by anarchist circles as an ascetic, martyr, and saint.

She lectured tirelessly on the virtues of anarchism and the importance of women's rights, forming the Ladies' Liberal League in 1893, a feminist study group standing for "non-acqui-escence to injustice." The sex question, she said, "is more intensely important to us than any other, because of the interdict which generally rests upon it, because of its immediate bearing upon our daily life, because of the stupendous mystery of it, and the awful consequences of it." One of her lifelong themes was the power of the individual will to affect society at large. After noting that she expected nothing from men as a class, Voltairine said her hope lies "in creating rebellion in the breasts of women." She was not invested in an organized movement of women, feeling that "independence can best be achieved by individual acts of rebellion." Women would be most effective "by making rebels wherever we can. By ourselves *living our beliefs.* 'Propaganda by the deed' is the favorite expression of a revolutionist. We are revolutionists. And we shall use propaganda by speech, deed, and most of all life—*being* what we teach." In her essay "The Gates of Freedom," written more than a hundred years ago, Voltairine suggested that a leaderless general strike against marriage and motherhood would challenge the traditional expectations of women, although she realized that such a spontaneous occurrence was unlikely.

This raises a question I've pondered for years: What will galvanize women into collective action? While it would be naive to minimize the complexities of our differences, it seems unwise as well to ignore our common experience of living under global patriarchy, or, as Marilyn French says so succinctly, "male supremacy backed by force," the style of which differs from one culture to the next, the objective remaining the same. What horrendous episode in the war on women will cause us to unite, to say finally, "No more!"? Or, acknowledging our phenomenal collective power, might we choose instead to gather in our strength and joy and vision to change the world?

Like many women, watching the Clarence Thomas hearings in 1991 when the Supreme Court justice nominee was accused of sexual harassment by former associate Anita Hill, I felt a shiver of possibility. Not because I felt optimistic about the hearing itself—clearly the process was humiliating and ultimately futile—but because for the first time in my memory, if only for a heartbeat, men were held publicly accountable for their demeaning treatment of women. Watching the men squirm and writhe, panic and lie, deny and attack as they were forced to hear story after story of the sexualized abuse of male power against women, I felt my head get hot. I began to imagine the impossible: a paradigm shift of the social order, men cast out of power and held accountable for their crimes against women, children, and the earth. Maybe this will not happen in concert, all at one time. Maybe I cannot wait until it does. Maybe this shift happens every time a women loves herself enough to draw the line.

Think that your soul is strong and will hold its way;
and slowly, through bitter struggle perhaps, the

strength will grow. And the foregoing of possessions for which others barter the last possibility of freedom, will become easy. At the end of life you may close your eyes, saying: "I have not been dominated by the Dominant Idea of my Age; I have chosen mine own allegiance, and served it. I have proved by a lifetime that there is that in man which saves him from the absolute tyranny of Circumstance, which in the end conquers and remoulds Circumstance,—the immortal fire of Individual Will, which is the salvation of the Future."

Voltairine de Cleyre, 1910

My next encounter was in Chicago. I landed at the airport on a chilly Sunday afternoon in March, rented a car, and drove to the Waldheim Cemetery where Voltairine was buried. Earlier that morning in South Bend, Indiana, I had pressed upon the woman driving me to the airport to find a place to buy flowers. She did, although displaying a bit of skepticism at my sanity when I explained excitedly why I wanted them—to place on Voltairine's grave. By this point, I was happily absorbed in my love affair with this brave and defiant soul, who believed in a future "in which gender would not serve as a defining characteristic for social roles, in which neither men nor women would feel restricted by sex," and a society where "human beings would cooperate as the leaf cooperates with the sun, as the moon with the tide, as lover with lover, asking no rules since none are needed." Or, as she succinctly put it on probably more than one occasion, "No government whatever."

Snow was still ankle-deep, and the overcast sky gave a somber tint to the twilight as I trooped through the oldest part of the enormous cemetery for over an hour. I didn't know how to find what I was looking for and became discouraged, wishing graves—like books in a library—were alphabetically arranged, or at least categorical: "anarchist-feminist women" here, "profiteering industrialist men" over there. Driving past the closed caretaker's cottage, I stopped to look for the attendant's Monday hours and found the clue I needed taped to the door: A small map to the grave sites of the Haymarket martyrs, whose false convictions and subsequent executions had sparked Voltairine's nascent devotion to anarchism, free thought, and individual liberty into a lifetime of service on behalf of those ideals. According to what I had read, she had asked to be buried near them.

Just a few feet from the huge, flag-marked memorial for the seven Haymarket men, and Emma Goldman's tall tomb with bronze portrait, was Voltairine's small headstone, only her name and the years of her birth and death engraved in the gray granite, nothing more. I placed the flowers and carefully planted a crystal over her heart then turned my thoughts inward.

At the turn of the last century, Voltairine de Cleyre was a visionary. She accurately predicted the unconscionable greed for "things" that has ravaged the earth since her death and pointed out possibilities for change in the fundamental ways we prioritize our choices. What would she think of this current era? Would she see any progress for women? Would she feel validated for her 20/20 foresight?

The century is turning again, and with it the millennium. I ask myself, what is the Dominant Idea of my age? Dare I stretch my imagination to name what I see? To create meaning? To assume my right to speak? To allow my head to get so hot, I become a torch blazing for that woman who believes, like I did, that she is alone? One day, I too will be dead in the ground like Voltairine, without the luxury to pose such questions. What did Volt say? *Dare: Write what others are afraid to write.*

In this critical time, what path do I choose? I find a description in Mary Daly's vocabulary, and I name myself *Hag:* "a Witch, Fury, Harpy who haunts the Hedges/Boundaries of patriarchy, frightening fools and summoning Weird Wandering Women into the Wild."[6]

I work the border, searching for hotheads. We look into the past and find our visions. We look into the future and ignite the curiosity in women's souls. In the present, we blaze. We are Many, and we are not boring.

Hothead To Do List

> ☞ Fall in love with an older woman: Read women's history! Begin to rebuild a connection to our glorious heritage. Read biographies, autobiographies, letters, and diaries—reading the actual words of the woman whenever possible. Discover her quirks and humanness as well as her achievements and legends. Some of my recent flings with "older women": Elsa Gidlow, Margaret Anderson, Zora Neale Hurston, Rebecca West, Emma Goldman, Georgia O'Keeffe. The possibilities, literally, are endless.

> ☞ Surround yourself with images of women, all ages, all races, all kinds of women. Begin to feed your hunger for the culture of women.

> ☞ At this writing the year 2000 is less than seven years away. Assuming the turn of the millennium will provoke

wide-sweeping change across the globe (and obviously this is already occurring), imagine what you would like to happen. Describe your vision—for yourself, your community, or the world—being as bold and specific as you can. When you know what you want, you can begin to create it.

🐦 Respect your own contribution to women's heritage: Keep a journal. No one else can tell your story. Don't leave out your chapter. Donate your journals to a women's archives after you join Voltairine.

🐦 Volt read about Mary Wollstonecraft, I read about Voltairine—the magic continues. Speak to a future hothead: Write a letter to a woman in the year 2093. What do you want her to know about our society, the condition of women, the spirit of our culture, yourself? Assume she will know as much about our era as you know about life in 1893.

NOTES

1   Dale Spender, *Women of Ideas (and What Men Have Done to Them)* (London: Thorsons, 1991), 23.

2   Text from postcard published by Helaine Victoria Press, a non-profit educational organization that for over ten years recovered and produced images of women on posters and postcards with accompanying text, introducing thousands of people to the vast heritage of women. This essay is dedicated to all the women who were Helaine Victoria Press; wherever you are, many thanks.

3   Quotations and information about Voltairine throughout this essay come from a variety of sourcebooks listed here in "Related Resources."

4   For a contemporary example of this technique, notice how many critics are "evaluating" Gloria Steinem's best-selling *Revolution from*

Within: The Book of Self-Esteem (New York: Little, Brown, 1992)—barely a nod to her broad and generous analysis of contemporary culture, with headlines and shredder pieces on her romantic liaisons.

5   For research assistance on virtually any subject, I recommend Celeste Tibbits's reasonable and inspirational consulting service, Point of Reference, 404–525–3042.

6   Mary Daly, with Jane Caputi, *The Wickedary* (Boston: Beacon Press, 1987).

Responses

This is a subject (that of strong female role models/mentors, both present and historic) that I have been thinking about over the last few months. It began with a journal entry about people, particularly women, whose lives have touched mine, those who have truly awakened me in some way. That's when I started what my husband refers to as my "Wall of Fame." It's just some clippings and photos tacked to the wall above my dresser. There is a photo and quotes from Isabel Briggs Myers and Gloria Steinem. There's something from my friend Tirzah Firestone and a postcard from you. There's a quote from Carl Jung and a picture of Paramhansa Yogananda. There's a card from my friend Graciela that says "It's time to find out who I am and stop letting others define me." Every day I look at these things, and I feel the support of these individuals who live their lives intelligently, passionately, and true to themselves. I feel a connection to each of them in some part of my own journey. They are all human and flawed and have struggled with the same hassles and attitudes as we all do. That makes me feel even more connected.

As I read your essay, I felt the way Voltairine de Cleyre entered your heart. That's how Isabel Briggs Myers affected me: like I could smell her brilliance, her determination and clarity of mind, like I couldn't get enough of her. The way I was awed by her work to encourage respect for diversity and her efforts with the idea of building world peace. All of this in a time (WWI) and a field (psychology) that were not exactly open to the ideas of a woman educated by her mother at home (make that a woman, period!). The essay reminded me that there are many more lives

to be touched by, and that by reading women's stories and pass-
ing them on to my daughters, maybe they, too, can find support
on their journeys.

Viola Rose Moriarty, Denver, CO

A couple of months ago I was violated in my workplace by a patriarchal wolf in an M.D.'s clothing—I was sexually harassed.
I'm sure I had been harassed before, but Anita Hill hadn't spo-
ken yet, and I was still only an intellectual hothead, with the ket-
tle on the back burner at that. As I agonized over how/when to
confront my oppressor, I could feel my righteous anger perme-
ate every cell of my body until it touched the deep well of
women's oppression. I understood something new about why
such violation is so hard to confront. My cells remembered.

We have so much information about our oppression and
our silencing and so little access to our tradition of talking
back. I wonder how differently I might have felt when I finally
chose to talk back if alongside the age-old memory of my oppression I had found the "broad, complex, and profound accomplishments of women" with equal strength. The fact that I
did not results some from inaction based on my own (happily
diminishing) bias about Women's Boring History; i.e., I
haven't taken the time to find Voltairine et al. But I must also
acknowledge the systematic exclusion of women's experience
that has often relegated our heroines to postcards and posters
(kudos nonetheless to the women who've managed to accom-
plish this!). I'm also beginning to understand something new
about why it is often the case that young women on college
campuses and in high school classrooms think feminism is
outmoded, unnecessary, and boring. As long as we have to

continue to re-create the energy for the movement in each successive generation, our cells will remember the oppression more readily and strongly than they will the tradition of our individual and collective hotheadedness.

To have to struggle so hard simply to find the context of our continuing activism is an insidious silencing. After all, context provides repetition and reinforcement. The historical information I met through my years of study had references to few (count 'em on one hand) women. The ones that I've met on my own since then I have difficulty remembering simply because there is no broader recognition of their contributions. I wonder how many of us would have remembered Napoleon in the absence of the male canon's relentless enforcement of his significance?

I think a national movement to create public shrines to our favorite Hotheads could be a step in the right direction!

Jan Arsenault, Santa Fe, NM

Codependency and the
Myth of Recovery

As a feminist and an adult child of alcoholics, I have taken great interest in the rising popularity of codependency as a way to describe unhealthy intimacy patterns. My journey as an ACA over the past few years affected me almost as profoundly as my personal awakening to feminism in 1974. But at first my journey as an ACA was on one track, my journey as a feminist on another. They were parallel. I did not see any overlap between the two until the term *codependency* arrived on the scene. The relationships among addiction, intimacy patterns, and how popular culture has interpreted them for women is the topic of this essay.

Scrutinizing the avalanche of information about codependency from a feminist perspective, I want to address the following questions:

ᛦ What exactly is codependency?

ᛦ Why is it particularly dangerous for women?

ᛦ Can we recover from codependency?

ᛦ Is there intimacy after codependency?

What is codependency? By linguistic standards, codependency is quite a new term, recognized and named less than twenty years ago. It commonly refers to a set of intimate behaviors and patterns often associated with the substance addiction of a partner or family member. The specific naming of the syndrome is important because, as with the term *battering*, which emerged in the mid-seventies, when we can name a set of behaviors, we can often recognize the pattern in our own lives. Naming, as the mythmakers knew when they gave Adam the privilege, is empowering magic. When codependency named this syndrome into visibility, many women recognized patterns in our lives and noticed that we were not alone.

The term *codependency* appeared for the most part simultaneously in the fields of addiction therapy and mental health. In the addiction field, codependency emerged when therapists noticed that alcoholics who had successfully gone through treatment often started drinking again after returning home. Soon therapists began to bring in the families for counseling on how to behave with the recovering addict. Within the Alcoholics Anonymous organization, the Al-Anon groups represent an awareness that the behavior of nonaddicted family members is affected strongly by the addiction. If patterns of family members do not change as the addict's habits change, therapists noted, the family setting often seems to work against the recovery process.

At the same time in the field of mental health, therapists noted the dynamic of the family system, which adapts itself to problems and restructures to insure efficient functioning. For instance, if a child becomes epileptic, the family quickly shifts into a stance designed to accommodate the unpredictable nature of the disease. In most cases the problem (whether epilepsy, alcoholism, or an absent parent) becomes the focus of the system. Family systems therapists treat the entire family, not just the "problem" member. An interesting term from this field is *fortress family,* describing family members' tendency to maintain tight, protective secrecy about problems, particularly incest, making it nearly impossible for outsiders to learn the reality.

In both fields codependency emerged gradually as a subtle but distinctive syndrome, a quiet and previously unnoticed context supporting a variety of more obviously destructive behaviors. Soon therapists responded by offering separate treatment for it, and now there are specialized clinics for treating codependency. The naming of this pattern acknowledges the presence of a condition that is deeply embedded in our culture and that cuts across sex, race, class, ability, and other differences.

Some Definitions of Codependency

The challenge of defining codependency is to describe accurately a behavioral phenomenon that is subtle, pervasive, and practiced with uncanny precision, inventiveness, and unconscious, virtually automatic obedience. The variety of the following definitions drawn from both addiction and family systems literature reflects early attempts to define the term. When I applied a feminist perspective to these efforts, I noticed some interesting implications.

"A specific condition that is characterized by pre-occupation and extreme dependence on a person, or object. Eventually, this becomes a pathological condition that affects the person in all other relationships" (Sharon Wegsheider-Cruse).

"Codependency is caused by those self-defeating, learned behaviors that diminish our capacity to initiate or participate in loving relationships" (Earnie Larson).

"A codependent person is one who has let another's behavior affect him or her, and who is obsessed with controlling that person's behavior" (Melodie Beattie).

"An emotional, psychological, and behavioral condition that develops as a result of an individual's prolonged exposure to and practice of a set of oppressive rules, rules which prevent the open expression of feeling as well as the direct discussion of personal and interpersonal problems" (Robert Subby).

The last definition caught my feminist attention. While codependency may be difficult to describe accurately, oppression is certainly something I recognize. Relating the two is the crux of this essay.

Subby is a family systems therapist, and as such he identifies the "set of oppressive rules" mentioned above as being characteristic of what he calls a "dysfunctional" family. According to his definition, codependency does not result specifically or solely from relating to an addict but rather from being reared in a dysfunctional family, which practices such rules as

- 🐦 Don't talk about your feelings.
- 🐦 Communication is best if it is indirect and triangulated.
- 🐦 Be strong, be right, be good, be perfect (unrealistic expectations).
- 🐦 Don't be selfish.
- 🐦 Do as I say, not as I do.
- 🐦 Don't rock the boat.

If we apply these typical characteristics, most American families might qualify as dysfunctional in that they practice similar oppressive rules whether or not a chemical addiction is present. Sharon Wegsheider-Cruse estimates that as many as 96 percent of families are dysfunctional. When I heard this statistic, the parallel tracks of my journeys as a feminist and an ACA suddenly crossed. An alarm sounded inside me, for I suspected I was hearing a reversal.

From feminism I have learned that reversal is a common patriarchal communications trick. Something described one way is in reality the opposite. The "strategic defense initiative," for example, is really the aggressive militarization of space. The "natural look" describes a style of makeup. I want to suggest that when 96 percent of American families display similar characteristics such as the oppressive rules outlined by Subby, what therapists describe as a "dysfunctional" family is clearly the norm. Perhaps what we have been told is dysfunctional is actually, for our culture, functional.

But what, then, is the family's function? What is the family supposed to be doing or producing? One obvious product, according to Subby, is codependency. Perhaps developing codependent behavior is the main function of the nuclear family, since it does so with such extraordinary efficiency. With cooperation from 96 percent of American families (plus or minus 4 percent) one might suspect this design is also deliberate.

While Subby describes the "dysfunctional" family as operating by "a set of oppressive rules," prolonged exposure to which results in behavior he describes as "codependent," feminist theorist and poet Adrienne Rich has described how the individual family unit under patriarchy serves as a training ground for dominance and subordination. From differing perspectives, both theorists observe that our earliest family models prepare us for relationships of unequal power. I suggest that codependency is a euphemism for internalized oppression and that its characteristics describe how dominance and subordination are acted out in intimate relationships.

Internalized oppression occurs when the subordinate takes in the beliefs of the dominator. The dominant group defines meaning, morality, and value, permeating society with images, institutions, structures, laws, and customs that reinforce these definitions. A white supremacist society defines people of color as inferior; a male supremacist society defines women as inferior. Eventually the subordinate group accepts the dominators' view as inevitable, as reality. This acceptance is convenient for the dominators, for at this point the members of the subordinate group begin to oppress themselves, vastly simplifying the enforcement of oppression.

The oppressive rules of the patriarchal family system train us to accept and expect the paradigm of dominance and subordination. Even the most benign of patriarchal families operates in a manner that cultivates the characteristics of *codependency,* a term that is much more acceptable than *internalized oppression,* which might encourage us to question authority or even to rock the boat.

So what are some of those characteristics? Perusing the current crop of self-help books on the subject, I find many checklists we can use to find out not just whether or not we are codependent but exactly how codependent we are, since the "disease" of codependency appears to be rampant. I have collapsed these characteristics into several pivotal qualities.

> *External referencing.* Always checking outside myself before making choices. I'm constantly monitoring my partner's behavior in order to "fix" or avoid conflict. This habit

separates me from my own feelings, needs, and wants—my self.

Martyrdom. Taking care of others while sacrificing my own needs, keeping score, suffering silently, feeling unappreciated and resentful, or denying my feelings completely.

Poor self-esteem. Feeling less than, unworthy, undeserving, incapable, unlovable.

Controlling behavior. Obsessing with my partner's behavior, passive aggression, manipulation by playing a victim, exposing vulnerability, or rescuing.

Demoralization. Feeling hopeless, despairing, helpless, futile, victimized, powerless.

Self-worth through being needed. If I define and value myself through taking care of my partner, I lose my sense of self when my partner goes into recovery, begins to get healthy, and doesn't need me. I may sabotage her/his recovery in order to maintain my self-worth.

When I look at these characteristics examining the power dynamic at play, I notice that they describe a woman perfectly socialized into a male-supremacist society or a person of color socialized into a white-supremacist society or any oppressed person in a system of dominance. Charlotte Davis Kasl refines the definition further, saying that codependency is "a predictable set of behavior patterns that people in a subordinate role typically adopt to survive in the dominant culture." Again, codependency is a logical consequence of the way we are trained to support a dominant-subordinate caste system.

As a woman in this culture, when I do not defer my needs to the needs of "the man," whether husband, father, brother, teacher, or boss, I am punished. Punishment may take the form of harsh words, a sullen look, withdrawal of affection, invalidation, a physical blow, rape, or death. I learn this early in life. I learn it so well that I forget I learned it. Deferring my needs for him and for others becomes my automatic choice. I become very creative at fulfilling the needs of others. I forget that I have needs. Life is easier when I don't have needs. In fact, when I am aware of my own needs, life under oppression becomes impossible. Finally my needs must become his needs.

Codependency is no accident, nor is it a disease or an individual character disorder afflicting us in a random manner, as popular self-help books and current therapeutic treatment would have us believe. A society of dominance trains the oppressed to be subordinate so that dominance may continue. For women this conditioning begins when we are born and extends throughout our lives via our family models, the images we see in the media, and interactions with institutions infused with male dominance. When we do not recognize the relationship codependency has to the culture, we risk falling prey to another aspect of our training in which we accept personal responsibility and blame for having somehow developed "unhealthy intimacy patterns." In a culture of dominance, the oppressed is always at fault.

On occasion the question is raised, What about men? Aren't they codependent, too? By viewing codependency as the practice of dominance and subordination, I see that in patriarchy men are trained to presume dominance over women, and society supports their presumption with institutionalized male privilege. So while some men may at times identify with the characteristics of "codependency," the neutrality of the term masks the unequal power between men and women. In a sexist society, many of the issues facing men who seek to improve their intimacy patterns revolve around the challenge of rejecting their inherited dominator role and learning to value and treat women as equals. How men and women act out their "codependency" is necessarily different and should be regarded and treated differently.

Can We Recover from Codependency?

Recovery is a term used to describe the phase in which an addict chooses to begin discarding addictive behavior in favor of previous nonaddicted behavior, for example, "I'm a recovering alcoholic" or "I'm in recovery from cocaine addiction." Now we find recovery being applied to codependency, such as "I'm in recovery from codependency." Many regard codependency as an addiction, in the same category as substance addiction, and the process by which we move into and out of it the same. Once again, my feminist self squirmed in discomfort. I felt recovery was somehow inappropriate when applied to codependency.

I resisted this discomfort. I enjoyed claiming the power of recovery; the word felt active, exciting, vital, moving out of the numbness of codependency's robotitude. In terms of physical addiction to a substance, recovery is accurate: To reclaim a healthier way of being, the addict decides to go back to a time when she or he was not addicted to the substance. But applied to codependency, the message is mixed. To say that recovery from codependency is possible implies that we can return to a previous time in our lives when we were healthier, when we related to our loved ones differently. It implies that there was a moment when something happened—we changed, we fell in with a bad crowd, or we took up bad ways—but now we are recovering what we lost. I suggest this is impossible.

Recovery from codependency is a myth. We cannot recover what we have never had. When we redefine codependency as internalized oppression, we see that as women we are conditioned to accept and practice our subordinate position from the moment we are born. As Subby has determined, the typical family system thoroughly trains us in this behavior. Born into patriarchy, we are groomed into codependency from the beginning of our lives. There was never a time that I was not codependent. To say I am "in recovery" is inaccurate, can lead to self-blame, and distracts me from noticing the influence of the culture of dominance. Here lies the danger to women of unscrutinized acceptance of the popular approach to codependency.

If I believe that challenging codependency is solely a matter of recovery, then I ignore the political context of oppression in which I live. I accept full responsibility, viewing codependency as an individual character disorder, something wrong with me personally. As such, appropriate treatment would be therapy, Twelve-Step programs, or at the very least a slew of self-help books. I will fix myself, "recover" my "sobriety," and then I will be capable of healthy intimacy. But when I try to "recover" from codependency, there is nowhere to go. Every road out leads back to codependency because my focus is limited to my personal inadequacy and does not include the culture that designs, maintains, rewards, and benefits from codependent behavior. With all due respect to the Twelve-Step programs of AA, these groups do little to develop a critical consciousness of the society that nurtures substance addiction and other forms of oppression. If I attempt to "recover" from codependency without this analysis, the oppressor remains invisible, my oppression a misnamed affliction, and I stay in a cul-de-sac of self-blame. Who does this benefit?

The subtle manipulation of our attention is one of patriarchy's greatest feats, keeping us distracted from focusing on the truths that would inspire us to action, revolt, resistance, and rage, much less vision, desire, felicity, and joy. Take the bestselling pop psychology book *Women Who Love Too Much.* The title is a classic reversal: Women are at fault again, this time for loving—what we've been reared to do—"too much." My question is, Where is the book for *Men Who Love Too Little?* Isn't this the real crux of the "problem"?

Anne Wilson Schaef's metaphor of the society as an addict is particularly mind-twisting. Leaving behind the "white male system" of her first book, *Women's Reality,* she has made addiction itself the focus, the pivotal demon, the monster at the core. But encouraging addiction and addictive behavior is only one of many tools the dominant caste uses to oppress. Violence, economic exploitation, homophobia, racism, and sexism are some others. Schaef's insistence on focusing on addiction as the main problem successfully renders invisible the context, a dominant-subordinate culture that creates many interlocking systems to perpetuate the imbalance of power. As Charlotte Davis Kasl observes, "These traits [of codependency] are taught and reinforced through institutions of family, education, church, traditional medicine, and mental health practices and philosophy in order to maintain patriarchy, capitalism, and hierarchy." I must take responsibility for my own decisions, yes, but I must also take into consideration that I live under oppression and that this is the context of my decision making. I am not to blame for my codependency.

Imagine what might happen if instead of saying, "I'm codependent," thousands of women were saying, "I'm oppressed." Imagine thousands of meetings in every city and town of the United States where women gathered once, twice, or three times a week to discuss their oppression, what caused it, what it feels like, how they collude with it, and what they might do about it. I venture to say this one slight shift in focus could galvanize women into radical, united action. Consciousness-raising groups, the discussion groups where women shared and compared their personal experiences, were a pivotal part of the excitement and power of feminism's second wave because they broke women's isolation from one another and enabled us to recognize the political oppression of all women. Might this be a reason for the propagandizing of codependency as a self-blaming double bind? In many ways this perspective keeps us from noticing our common problems and prohibits us from seeing the political implications of our conditioning, the potential for personal empowerment, political action, or magic. I believe that by using a combination of self-examination and social consciousness, we can discover effective ways to challenge both our internalized oppression and the culture of dominance that surrounds us.

Is There Intimacy Beyond Codependency?

If we cannot recover from codependency, what can we do? Leaving behind the familiar prison of dominance and subordination, we enter the wilderness of intimacy and begin a process of *discovery*. To move beyond my internalized oppression, I must be willing to examine my own behavior and attitudes, find the roots of them in my past, and become aware of how my unique conditioning fits into and colludes with the overall design of the culture of dominance. I must be prepared also to explore entirely unfamiliar terrain: loving relationships among equals.

Without illusion, lying, indirect communication, passive aggression, manipulation, self-sacrifice, projection, the need to control or rescue, persecution, codependency, dominance and subordination, what is intimacy, anyway? What does it feel like, look like, act like? How do we begin to connect with one another at the level of our essential selves? What are the rules for intimacy between and among self-loving, self-aware beings? We have no models, no guidelines, no environment of support. We must create them.

Responses

Men aren't the only oppressors. Whites aren't the only oppressors. Women oppress, too. Maybe the reason we women revel in our caretaking, nurturing roles is that the children, pets, plants, old people, etc., that we care for are, in our minds, beneath us, as we are beneath men. It's one-upwomanship.

My thought is that maybe everyone likes being the oppressor now and then. I've seen it in the sibling rivalry between my children, and I've seen it in the relationship between my two dogs (both female), and I'm beginning to notice it between me and the dogs.

P. D., Atascadero, CA

I address the subject of self-neglect as a guide for a person wondering if their behavior is their acting out "old messages" or if they are being polite and kind. Not very long ago I was at a Twelve-Step meeting where the question came up again. The topic was, Do I stop and help someone who is carrying an armful of packages, or is that being codependent?

If I can be of help to you in any way and that attention is not self-neglecting, I am not being codependent. I am being kind and responsible. If I have to go out of my way to be kind and responsible and I can do this without neglecting myself, this is admirable. However, I caution clients to watch out, because one of the most prevalent ways we get strokes for ourselves is to bend over backward for others. In an awareness exercise, I had someone bend over backward. The only direction they could see in this position was backward. In looking backward we see and hear only familiar messages, many of which are indeed oppression.

Suzanne Bowers, Asheville, NC

Let's stop sugarcoating the patriarchy. I support the current atomized forms of recovery because it is a start . . . but I am upset that intelligent people choose to close their eyes to other realms of the recovery process. I am disturbed that activists refuse to incorporate spirituality in their political movements. I feel isolated that so few people understand how a conflation of the two processes is absolutely essential to revolutionary change and species survival.

What am I to do? You can't unring a bell. I can't just tune out my deeper levels of pain and concomitant deeper goals of planet healing. I will not silence the voice within me that knows working through feelings demands more than simply working through those feelings of a personal nature. Where can I find the support I need? With my consciousness where it is, being with groups of people who refuse to deal with the deeper concerns, who will not or cannot understand why saying "God" is antithetical to true, deep healing, who turn their backs on oppressive political realities, much less patriarchy—where can I turn to for effective support?

Well, I've started a women's study group. We're starting out with Sonia Johnson and Merlin Stone . . . excited to read Mary Daly, Marilyn Frye, Sarah Hoagland, and your essays . . . this small group of women, I feel, is going to help me negotiate life on a deeper level. I believe radical feminism is both a spiritual and a political belief system. I hope that in this group my spirituality can find a place of nurture without my having to compromise my political integrity. The Twelve-Step program just does not do that for me.

Cathleen McGuire, New York, NY

Families by their very nature, that is, adult-child, are relationships of unequal power. Adults are supposed to be dominant and children subordinate. In fact child development professionals talk about the need children have to know the family's set of rules and say that rules are helpful to children.

Yet children are supposed to grow up, and adolescence is that revolution whereby the child does try to get out of the subordinate role. Perhaps part of the problem is not only the original "oppressive" rules but also the way the rules don't change as the child grows. Adult children of alcoholics who are stuck in the old oppressive rules begin recovery by learning new rules that are a better match for happiness and intimacy. Perhaps no one has ever really grown up anywhere.

E. K., Columbus, OH

Your article confirmed a gut-level reaction I was having as I sat in ACA meetings. My intuition was saying, There is another issue here; something else is going on besides being an adult child raised in an alcoholic family. Part of why I became suspicious was because the men were discussing how shut down, isolated, unable to connect they were, and the women were talking about giving too much, having no sense of self, being used, abused, and abandoned, . . . sounded like sex-role stereotyping to me.

M. J. S., Seattle, WA

As I challenge my codependency, I find that I fit in less among my family and my co-workers. . . . I am encouraged to know that other women are thinking along the same lines, because I do wonder where I will fit in if someday I am no longer codependent. What happens to the sane people in an insane world? In a world where power to control others is valued, martyrdom is encouraged, and demoralization is accepted, will I, ironically, go crazy?

I do not see your point about the traditional treatment of codependency involving self-blame. I do see the relationship between codependency and oppression, and I see the concept of "recovery" from codependency as a self-empowering process. The idea that we can get out of it by assertion of our will does not imply, to me, that we got ourselves into it. Rather, the only way to break out of a process as institutionalized as codependency is willfully, and I cannot imagine that anyone who is as in touch with their true self as someone who is challenging codependency must surely be, could fail to recognize it for the internalized oppression that it is.

S. G., Dallas, TX

It is especially easy for us in the U.S. to get trapped into taking sole and total responsibility for our "shortcomings" and "unhealthy behavior." Our cultural myth, deeply embedded in the U.S. psyche, is one of rugged individualism. So it is relatively easy to unquestionably accept at a deep level that we alone are the cause and we somehow have to fix our individual, alone self.

Eileen B. Cohen, Albuquerque, NM

Bradshaw describes the dysfunctional family as one in which there are no boundaries, no one in the family is who they appear to be. There is no mutually established delineation of where I stop and another family member begins. This is another piece of the training-since-birth that conditions women to life in the patriarchy. . . . No one can become aware of a boundaryless condition (an oppressed condition) or establish needed boundaries or realize they have a right to set limits . . . without some experience of being present to themselves, coming to or waking up, as it were, for the first time, witnessing her own experience. . . .

I think recovery is a possibility, a back-to-the-future proposition—a reclaiming of bodies, Earth, and earthiness (our "lustiness" and "elemental passion," in the words of Mary Daly), which we indeed once had (although I don't know, I wasn't there) and then . . . a stepping off into the wilderness.

When I am my best self, when my certainty about my own experience is high, when I am present, when I am validated and set free by the words and voices of my sisters, I have moments of perfect boundaries. I confess they are only moments and that they are sometimes broken by something as slight as a memory of an invalidation.

J. J., Atlanta, GA

The idea that codependency is an internalized process in all of us is pretty depressing. If codependency is the product of family life, the very basis of our society, then does this mean we should disband the family as it exists and live in some other way? Should we switch to a communal system, as some have suggested? Can we devise a way to live our lives without being either the leader (dominator) or follower (subordinate) of any system we exist in?

Although I have not lived communally, my experience with cooperative endeavors is that some one person is usually the moving force, using the impact of their personality to make sure their ideas (which they are convinced are the best) prevail. Cooperative efforts take three times as long as any other way to get something accomplished. Sometimes everyone wants their ideas to prevail, other times no one really cares but feels they should have input anyway. Dominator-subordinate systems are often more efficient when time is limited. What can we do about that problem?

And then how does this knowledge translate to my everyday life? I work as a secretary in an office where the patriarchal model is embedded. Women here do not get hired for anything other than to support the men. Because I have a daughter to raise, I don't feel free to choose a more sympathetic life-style while she is in school. Besides, I like having money to go to workshops and to buy books. I am left with the necessity of accommodating myself to the system in power. And therein lies the seed of our dilemma. We continue to live in a slave society, lowering our eyes and dipping our knee to get along and to avoid drawing hostility. The more we realize our oppression, the harder it gets to go out every day and dissemble. How can we live outside the system and still survive?

Shirley K., Northville, MI

You say, "Men who love too little, isn't this the real core of the problem?" Well, it is surely the core of a lot of problems. It surely isn't something that I find I can fix or even want to put my energy into fixing. And I wouldn't say that it is, because of that, the core of my problem. "To oppose something is to maintain it" (Ursula K. LeGuin). I wouldn't deny that the System is a setup, that the game is fixed, that it just isn't fair. My problem is how to grow, how to get surer and healthier and stronger and more solid and radical and witchy and dykey and outrageous, and to stay true to my own self; to live honorably and ethically according to my values and not to fall into the self-sabotaging patterns I learned in my first thirty-four years and that still call out to me.

I am responsible to that and I address it, and it is the root of my spiritual life. Naming the oppressors is useful, as I've said. I need to keep a keen eye out for the ones in my head and the ones outside. But men who love too little can do what they will. I avoid spending my energy on them, even too much of my rage. . . . I have better things to do.

Leslita, Archer, FL

I'd like to believe that I was once free from the social constraints I've memorized. And maybe this explains why the myth of recovery is so popular: It promises us a "return" to an Edenlike state of being that, much as we might wish we'd once had, may never have existed. Yet how much easier it is to keep believing in it. The fact that we may never have been there in the first place can then become another secret that we collude with ourselves to keep from knowing. . . .

What can we use as an image to take the place of recovery? I like your word, *discovery*. People trying out alternatives to co-dependent behaviors are showing courage in exploring new territory and are discoverers in a true sense of the word. I imagine it to be like uncovering an archaeological site where a peaceful, Goddess-worshiping society lived and learning what it might have been like to grow up in such a society.

Monique Wittig wrote: "Try to remember. Or, failing that, invent" (*Les Guerilleres*). The myth of recovery keeps us trying and trying to remember. We need a paradigm for "post-codependency" that encourages us also to invent—because we'll surely need to do that.

S. A., Durham, NC

The Wilderness of Intimacy:
Control and Connection

Intimacy is not a candlelit dinner for two. It cannot be contrived. Nor is it automatic, romantic, or necessarily even comfortable. Intimacy is a wilderness of sudden unpredictability, a dynamic of awareness, assertion, and courage. Intimacy occurs when I notice I am alive.

This essay explores some observations along a certain trail in Intimacy that I have marked Control and Connection. Please bring your compass, flashlight, calamine lotion, and trail mix.

My lover and I are walking by the bay after midnight. The moon is full. High over our heads, a tropical breeze pushes the palm trees around. We walk with our arms around each other's waists. The moment is precious. My lover is saying how much she values our relationship, how she misses me when we are apart, how she loves me. I am saying nothing. As I listen, I find I don't believe her. I remember recent hard words between us, how scared I felt. I do not trust her words now. I do not trust her. What does she mean by "love"? I notice she has fallen silent. She says, "What are you thinking?" Her question causes me, invisibly, to panic.

What is intimacy? Without my old unhealthy patterns, I barely recognize my intimate relationships. Dictionary open and romance aside, I find a clue in the root word *intimus*, meaning "innermost layer." Basically, then, intimacy means sharing from the innermost part, in a relationship marked by close association.

So if I am being intimate with you, I am sharing from my innermost part. I notice no qualifiers in this definition, nothing to say that this close association is necessarily good. Or healthy. Or secure. Or even voluntary. To know these things I need context, I need to find out how the power between us is disbursed. "Sharing from the innermost part" sounds important, though, certainly something I would want to do carefully, selectively, and well—whatever the context. Surely I had some kind of training for this profound activity. I scan my memory. Didn't I have intimacy lessons somewhere along the way, between basketball practice and piano lessons? Perhaps intimacy was part of my "higher" education.

No, like most people, my first close associations were with family, and here is where I learned to be intimate. This may not, however, be such a great setting for learning healthy intimacy skills. The nuclear family model under patriarchy, including the occasional benevolent version, institutionalizes sexism. Current laws are slight modifications of the assumption that the man is the "head," he owns the woman and children. We see this in states that do not recognize marital rape, and when fathers are awarded custody of children even when evidence of sexual abuse is present. Family sex-role stereotyping and power abuse by parents are our first encounters with the principles of dominance and subordination. Our earliest intimate experiences prepare us to accept, create, and practice relationships of unequal power.[1] I notice I have learned this lesson well.

If I tell her the truth about what I am thinking, we may argue again. There has been tension each time we've talked of the conflict. I could lie and say, "Nothing." Or say, "I was thinking of how much I've missed you." Say anything but the truth. The truth might hurt her. The truth hurts me. I'm afraid if I tell her the truth, she'll leave me. I'm afraid the truth will separate us.

Habits of dominance and subordination are instilled so perfectly into my psyche that I can detect them only with the most intentional, conscientious scrutiny, and even then, euphemistic terms like *codependency* keep me from seeing the context of my struggle. With the help of a feminist perspective, I can see the thorough precision of patriarchal conditioning, how it has infiltrated even my most private exchanges. There is a method to their madness. But why is the patriarchy even interested in this arena of my life? Why does patriarchy want to keep me from being intimate? As long as I conform to its values in my public actions, which can be achieved through intimidation, what difference does it make what I do in private with my beloved? Is nothing sacred?

Actually intimacy is not what patriarchy seeks to prohibit. Reflecting on the fact that intimacy is not necessarily positive or negative, that it is "close association" and "sharing from the innermost part," I note that it is also a prerequisite for access to the subordinate, and thus essential for the dominator's maintenance of control. Intimacy is necessary. Intimacy allows invasion. Incest. Brainwashing. Torture. Abuse. Violence can be extremely intimate. The patriarchy needs intimacy. What it must do is to dictate what happens in the intimate sphere, for this is also the context for connection. This possibility is threatening to patriarchal order, for connection can reveal the illusions that sustain domination.

Patriarchy, a worldview that advocates a dominant-subordinate caste system, depends on separation and estrangement for its survival. Obviously, in order to oppress properly, subordinate groups and individuals must be clearly identified so they can be separated from the dominators. After all, one needs to know whom to oppress. But the subtle levels of separation and estrangement are equally crucial to the maintenance of patriarchal control.

The dominator must separate different subordinate groups from each other to discourage unity and awareness. No networking allowed. In the late 1960s, for example, the potential coalition between the civil rights movement and the antiwar movement posed a particular threat to the dominant regime. Steps were taken, in fact, to prevent this connection.

Further, individuals within subordinate groups must feel isolated as individuals. For instance, women are separated from one another by the societal insistence that to be valued a woman must be "with" a man, significantly minimizing her intimate contact with other women and encouraging her to devalue what contact she does have with women.

Finally, a successful patriarchy requires that each individual must feel estranged from one's self. This is accomplished by self-hatred, enforced by internalized oppression. We can experience this as alienation, low self-esteem, emptiness, lack of purpose, and futility, creating an internal receptivity to authoritarian rule. This last level of separation may be the most important, for when I hate myself, I will accept abuse and allow my subordination. When I love myself, my energy is no longer automatically available to the dominant culture. I claim it for myself.

The purpose of patriarchal interference in intimacy is to prohibit connection in our close associations. We have seen how "codependency"—that intimate epidemic—is an obsession with control. Under patriarchy the subordinate must control the dominator or die, while the dominator controls the subordinate for sport. Either way, authentic connection is impossible, and the patriarchal order is intact. In our intimacies, then, we have been taught to substitute control for connection.

If I lie to her, I can make sure we do not ruin this precious moment by arguing. I can wait until another time, a more appropriate time of my own choosing, to tell her of my fears, of my mistrust. Until then, I will know about my scared feelings and she will not. She will think nothing is wrong. If I lie to her, I am putting myself in a dominant position by choosing to withhold information that is influencing our relationship.

So here I am, in the privacy of my own relationships, apparently of my own volition, practicing oppression and calling it love. My learned "intimacy" skills actually prohibit me from connecting with others, and especially with myself. However, I am quite capable of creating complex illusions and constructing elaborate projections that keep us apart while I appear to be deeply and earnestly engaged. What does this look like in a typical relationship? I call it the Multiple Mask Syndrome (MMS).

I want you to love me. But because of my self-hatred, I am afraid if you really know me, you couldn't possibly love me. I imagine, then, the kind of person I believe you would love, and I create a mask of this idealized version of myself and always wear it around you.

I want to love you. I want to believe you are the one I've been waiting for all my life. I idealize you so that you will resemble this person, and I project this mask onto you. For a long time, I only notice things about you that resemble the mask.

In the meantime you are doing the same thing: You wear a mask that looks like the person you believe I would love, and you project an idealized mask onto me. Individually we begin to believe we are the masks, and the deceit extends to ourselves. We are many masks having a very intense relationship, but we are not connecting. Our intimacy skills help us create and sustain these illusions that keep us from knowing the truth about ourselves and each other.

The Multiple Mask Syndrome is based on self-hatred: I am afraid if I let you know my true self, you would hate her like I do. MMS is maintained by lying. I lie to you about who I am, I lie to myself about who you are. I begin to believe these lies, and the exchange gets ever more complex. This happens on an unconscious level. The masks go on automatically. The lies are much easier to tell than the truth, and sound more real. The energy of the lie directs our intimate path.[2]

Without my masks of lies, I feel like things are out of control. If I am not controlling you or being controlled by you, I don't feel like anything is happening between us. I don't know what is supposed to happen next, and I can't predict what will. Without the security of my old patterns formed by patriarchal conditioning, I feel awkward, scared, panicky. What happens if I take off my mask? What happens if I look at you without yours? What happens if we simply present ourselves in our truth? I believe this is the threshold to the wilderness of authentic, positive intimacy beyond even "equal" power, to a place where power simply is.

She is waiting for my answer. I have only a moment to decide, or my silence will decide for me. I breathe deeply, monitor my tone of voice, reach for gentleness, and say, "I was feeling scared. I was remembering the argument. I was thinking that I don't trust you right now. I feel sad about this."

Connection asks me to be alive in the moment, to come maskless and open. Connection asks me to know myself, and to be willing to know you. Anything might happen in this wilderness of truth. Windstorms, lightning, poison ivy, rapids, a rainbow, a deer. You might like me, just as I am. I might even like myself. I can come prepared to this wilderness, I can train and practice for it, I can stay alert, but I cannot control what will happen. Control prevents connection.

Connection to what? A fundamental principle of a feminist view is the belief that all of life is interconnected. What I do influences you. What you do influences me. When I choose to tell the truth, I create the opportunity for you to know me. I learn I am not alone, and I feel my power. I wake up. I feel the urge of loving change, and I choose to move with it. I am connected to life. I am life. I notice I am alive.

We stop walking. Our talk is tentative and tender. Painful. Suddenly we are intimate. We are sharing from our deepest selves. We are telling the truth. We see each other, know each other. We are connecting. We are loving. This is what happens next.

NOTES

1   bell hooks, "The Significance of Feminist Movement," in *Feminist Theory: From Margin to Center* (Boston: South End Press, 1984).

2   Diana M. Grove, personal conversation with author, September 1989.

Responses

I'd like to talk about the masks we wear.

I was born before WWII and raised by parents born just after the turn of the century. The things you are talking against were the natural way of life to them. We were a farm family. My dad worked long hours and didn't say much, so my mother was the raiser, the teacher, the enforcer for all but major "crimes."

We quickly learned not to "talk back." Mom couldn't bear contradiction in any form. (Do you think it's strange that I married a man the very same?)

I work in a bank.

My life *is* a mask. And I'm not sure that's a bad thing. If I said exactly what I thought all the time I would not have a job, a husband (in fact I'd probably be dead—you notice how often men are killing their women instead of letting them go these days?), a speaking relationship with any of my children, etc., etc.

My husband and I have been married for thirty-four years. No, we don't have the intimacy of complete sharing, but we do have an intimacy of shared experiences and children and grandchildren (the best yet!) and knowing about everything you can know about another person. I figure I'm in this "till death do us part. . . ." I promised "for better or for worse," so some of it is worse.

Thank heavens, I have my diary, where I can release some of the pent-up hostilities from my system. And I can keep track of my life. You don't know how hard it is to get beneath the mask when I write, or how dismally I fail sometimes, but I keep trying.

Now, I have a question. Why is it always easier to take the masks off and tell complete strangers things that you wouldn't think of telling your nearest and dearest?

E. M., Wheeler, WI

Connection is looking toward my partner and feeling that the secrets are few. Mysteries will always exist and should never be lost, and I consider them differently. Connection is being and feeling accepted without being made to acknowledge an inventory of changes to work for in the future.

Connection vs. Control: There is no connection when there is control. Control is a symptom of insecurity. It will ultimately lead to resentment. I have always known that I could never connect with someone who wasn't my match. It takes a strong personality to enter my life because if I do fall into a controlling frame of mind and if I do succeed, I am left with a distaste for the individual who I have dominated. When feeling secure, I have no motivation to control. When feeling secure, I connect and I share. Yet a danger does exist. At times when I try to share, if the other does not receive my sharing for what it is but interprets it as an exercise of control, then the connection will never materialize. So it is not enough to feel secure and want to connect. She or he whom you are trying to reach must be as strong as you are. Reality is not as strong as perception. Perception all too often swallows reality and spits it out in a new, unrecognizable form.

Maytee Aspuro, Milwaukee, WI

I just had another excruciating interchange with my (male) manager; I was so tired of making excuses for my not getting along with him. My fault for being intolerant of his power moves; my fault that I chose to work for another withholding, patriarchal type in the most patriarchal environment I could find. The only thing that is still my fault is that I am still there. So as of January 1 I will be out of there. You gave me back a power base I had lost track of recently and gave me the courage to make the break.

Shirley K., Northville, MI

I'm unsure whether it is possible to have safe intimacies with those who are not working to change their patriarchal conditioning. Intimacy is a mutual awareness, a mutual act. You cannot have intimacy with someone who chooses not to be intimate with you. You can self-disclose, but you cannot achieve the empowerment and feelings, the sensation of intimacy. Self-disclosure can be safe, but self-disclosure doesn't necessarily have to be a sharing, as intimacy is. Intimacy involves a mutual openness: self-disclosure requires only one to act. The other can participate or not. Self-disclosure is potentially a vulnerable state to put yourself into if it is not coupled with intimacy. Vulnerability places safety in jeopardy.

. . . I agree that we must engage in positive forms of intimacy, to learn about each other, to connect, to create the bonds that will free us from domination and oppression. My problem is how to do this. Every day we're confronted (that word chosen specifically) with control: others who try to control us. It is difficult to try to connect when the other is trying to control. It creates incredible vulnerability and the potential for a lot of negative emotional (or rational/irrational) engagements. I want intimacy. I have tasted it and know it to be sweet and warm. It is full of energy, of crisp air, brilliant skies, sudden excitement, peaceful contentment. But where to begin? Feminist dyke that I am, I believe the best place to start is with us, with our community.

Kate Morrow, East Falmouth, MA

Orchids in the Arctic:

The Predicament of Heterosexual Feminism

W hen we undertake a difficult task, our chances of success are increased if we clearly understand the level of difficulty involved so that our efforts can equal the challenge. For instance, if we attempt to raise orchids in the arctic, we would be well advised to appreciate the effects of the frigid culture on the fragile blossoms we want to grow. We cannot forget or deny that the arctic climate is dangerous, even deadly, for orchids, typically a tropical flower. And so it is in the case of heterosexual feminism.

Women do not live in a benign or even neutral society. Our society is prejudiced against us in the most fundamental ways imaginable, and in many ways we cannot dare imagine. Most of us move through this culture in denial of its prejudice because the reality of it is too horrible to bear. The basis for this prejudice is male supremacy, and the practice of it is woman-hating. We tend to avoid naming the condition so specifically because of the absurd injustice it implies: a caste system based on gender. Feminism teaches us ways to recognize the existence of this prejudice in institutions, systems, and individuals around us; to understand how we have internalized the prejudice; and finally to acknowledge that our private, personal relationships are affected by this prejudice. Yet whether or not we call ourselves feminists, we know this caste system exists. All of us, women and men alike, are conditioned to conform to this culture. Men are trained to be dominators; women are trained to be subordinates. No one is exempt.

To survive in a misogynist environment, a woman must learn how to protect innate female power from a society designed to destroy it. After she learns to recognize and avoid male violence in its many forms, a woman's capacity for self-love blossoms, and her female power begins to thrive—creativity, vitality, and confidence emerge, along with a refusal to subordinate herself to male power. But heterosexual women choosing this path face particular challenges, for the cultural resistance to female power is most extreme in the more intimate realms. Even women who do not choose men as partners must occasionally relate to fathers, brothers, sons, male friends, and colleagues. Essentially, then, the predicament of heterosexual feminism is this: What kind of intimate, individual relationship is possible between the oppressor and the oppressed?

Over the years, from a heterosexual and now a lesbian perspective, I have pondered these questions. Can orchids grow in the arctic? Possibly, providing a woman has adequate resources and information and she prepares herself appropriately for the relentless hostility of the arctic climate. So button up your overcoats. In the spirit of scientific inquiry, I want to explore the predicament of heterosexual feminism and the floricultural potential of frozen tundra.[1]

FIELD NOTE

What is the orchid?

Female power.

What is the arctic?

Male supremacy, woman-hating, patriarchy.

What is the climate?

Hostility and aggression, expressed by males to females.

What is the culture/soil?

Frozen tundra: the practice of dominance and subordination.

The Prevailing Winds: Heterosexuality

Heterosexuality may be the norm in our society, but there is no way to know if it is actually normal. If you currently identify yourself as heterosexual, think back to the first moment you realized that you were heterosexual. Possibly it was not until you became aware of homosexuality. As children, most of us never questioned our sexual orientation. We followed the cues, both subtle and obtuse, telling us that the opposite sex was attractive, compelling, and correct for our affectional partners. Some of those cues were obvious, such as the model set by most parents. Others were more discreet, such as advertisements using sex-role stereotypes. At any rate, we all got the dominant culture's message: Hetero = YES, Homo = NO, and the majority of us never examined our choice. But if in fact heterosexuality were the only option perceived, can we call it a choice at all?

Until we elect to take over the job, the dominant culture constructs our reality and forms our values. Our sexual orientation is not immune or exempt from this process. The belief that one's heterosexual "preference" is natural is purely speculative. Society has a sexual agenda for us. Our choice is made in response to it. We cannot know what our choice of sexual activity would be if left to our natural desires in an unbiased culture. As feminists, we come to understand that while heterosexuality may in fact be a natural choice for many women, when practiced under misogynist rule, it can also function as a tool of oppression.

Adrienne Rich has observed, "To take the step of questioning heterosexuality as a 'preference' or 'choice' for women—and to do the intellectual and emotional work that follows—will call for a special quality of courage in heterosexually identified feminists, but I think the rewards will be great: a freeing up of thinking, the exploring of new paths, the shattering of another great silence, new clarity in personal relationships."[2]

Sarah Hoagland distinguishes the use of heterosexuality as a tool of oppression by using the term *heterosexualism*. This set of practices, she explains, is not limited to choices around sexual partners but extends to an entire way of living that includes the economic, political, and emotional aspects of relationships, "in which both men and women have a part. . . . Heterosexualism is a way of living . . . that normalizes the dominance of one person in a relationship and the subordination of another. As a result, it undermines female agency." She defines agency as "the power to act."[3]

In order to understand the implications of heterosexuality as a political tool, I find it useful to compare certain elements of the racial caste system to the gender caste system. The construction of white supremacy is similar in many ways to that of male supremacy. There are two groups polarized into dominators and subordinates; there is a vast, interconnected system of overt and covert coercion to maintain the hierarchy. Yet enforcing the caste system of gender differs from enforcing the caste system of race in at least one important aspect. To maintain white supremacy, the dominant caste prefers segregation in housing and intimate partnerships. De facto or de jure, whites claim certain neighborhoods, consigning people of color to other areas. Sexual relations between racial castes are discouraged (unless they are expressions of the dominators' privileged access). But in the gender caste system, members of the subordinate class of women are socially coerced to take a "partner" of the dominant class of men. Each woman then has an individual monitor, is under constant surveillance, and is subject to unlimited access. Under male supremacy, heterosexuality insures that women are, in essence, intimately colonized by the dominant class.[4]

Having been thoroughly trained to subordinate her needs to his, the heterosexual woman has few opportunities to experience her own power or to feel the surge of energy that comes from connection to other powerful women. The impact on possible unified action of women is devastating. In this way, we see how heterosexuality functions as the fundamental institution of male supremacy.

FIELD NOTE

Prevailing winds are constant, frigid,
fifty miles per hour from due north.

Learning from Inuits: Primary Relations with Men

Inuits are people who are indigenous to the arctic. To pursue our desire to raise orchids in our metaphorical arctic, it would behoove us to observe Inuit customs and tactics that demonstrate a few simple principles:

- ☞ You cannot deny that the arctic is hostile to entities accustomed to a warm climate.
- ☞ You cannot pretend the arctic is the tropics.
- ☞ You must accept the arctic's constancy if you are to survive.

If you understand these principles, you can learn how to meet your basic survival needs. If you do not, you will gradually freeze to death and not even know it.

The cultivation of female power under male supremacy takes a similar level of consciousness. To prepare for our own arctic venture, some principles to remember might be:

- ☞ We live in a male supremacist society.
- ☞ Male supremacy is aggressively and deliberately hostile to women and the expression of female power.
- ☞ It is within this context that we form and practice relationships.

Inevitably, individual men are microcosms of the larger misogynist climate. Interaction with men is hazardous for women because men who are born and reared in a male-supremacist, woman-hating culture such as ours have to some extent internalized those same values. At some level, men actually believe in them. Some men are nicer than others; some men are more violent than others; some men believe their superiority to women is innate; other men eschew their gender privilege as false and constructed; still others are homosexual, people of color, or physically disabled. But all these men live daily in a society that is designed to benefit them on the basis of their gender. They will act out of their conditioning of male privilege unless they have consciously chosen to select other behaviors, just as women will act out their subordination until they reject it in favor of self-loving behavior. In this way, most of us are robots, mindlessly obedient to the culture of dominance and subordination.

"When women climb out of their roles and challenge the male role, men feel very threatened. They get scared. They'll feel like they are gonna die or they feel like they have to kill to defend themselves. Males are conditioned to equate power with the ability to conquer, to kill, dominate, exploit, oppress, annihilate" (Charlie Kreiner).[5]

Generally a woman coming to feminist consciousness—that is, a woman actively practicing self-love—will gradually remove herself from subjection to overt, grotesque woman-hating, such as a battering relationship or a psychologically and emotionally terrorizing one, economic dependency that is being used to control and manipulate her, sexual harassment on the job, or discrimination on the basis of gender. Then, if heterosexual, she begins to choose her intimate male partners more carefully, searching for men who are not threatened by female power. Trudging through miles of frozen tundra, she looks for a site for her greenhouse.

FIELD NOTE

Inuits have igloos. Orchids need greenhouses.

Assessing the Climate: Questions from the Field

To understand what is necessary to cultivate the orchid of female power in the arctic land of misogyny, we must carefully
observe and realistically assess the climate itself. Women who
attempt this feat return to the tropics with many questions,
some of which I will address here.

☞ *Are men conscious that their behavior is frequently patroniz-*
   ing, abusive, controlling, violent, or hateful to women?

Probably not. If they are, we must certainly avoid them, particularly if they have a weapon. The question of men's consciousness is frequently raised in our attempts to explain
inexcusable behavior. We think, "Surely, if he understood the effect of what he is doing, he wouldn't do it," and this reasoning is
somehow soothing to us. When such behavior has taken place
in the company of others, we are sometimes compelled to turn
to our friends and assure them (and ourselves), "He's not really
like this." The man who practices woman-hating with conscious
intent is much more predictable than the one who is reacting
unconsciously to the culture's directives. There can be no mis-
taking or excusing the deliberate male supremacist, and thus he
can be easily avoided without confusion or guilt.

It's the nice men who allow us to slip into denial, setting ourselves up to be hurt. A chilling rule coined during my early for-
ays into the arctic is "If he can hurt you, he will"—meaning, if I
go unprotected into an encounter or relationship with a man,
he will eventually hurt me in some way, because that is what he
is trained and directed by the culture to do. As harsh as it may
sound, when I remember this rule and act accordingly, I find
that my interactions with men improve remarkably. Compassionate men can appreciate that in a culture such as ours, a

woman's trust must be respectfully earned.

FIELD NOTE

The Hawaiian shirt is not appropriate attire for the frigid zone: we must pull out the oiled and fur-lined sealskin parka.

🐦 *My father/husband/dentist is different/supportive/"more feminist than I am." Aren't there exceptional men?*

No. The myth of the exceptional man is a product of denial. As stated earlier, none of us has escaped the conditioning of the dominant culture, which is male supremacist and woman-hating. (Tiresome, isn't it?) To pretend that a few of us have escaped destroys our only opportunity to create authentic relationships that require men to confront and change their basic conditioning. Obviously, some men do distinguish themselves by working actively for gender justice and challenging male power abuse in themselves and other men. Their efforts make them seem exceptional, but it is precisely because they acknowledge and give up their unjust privilege.

FIELD NOTE

Always close the greenhouse door.

🐦 *Are men educable?*

Certainly. This is evident because they have learned to practice dominance so well. The more pertinent question might be, Can men be re-educated? And my observation is that some of them can. Be wary, however, of men who are motivated to change solely to save a relationship. Their changes are superficial and will dissolve when the relationship appears secure. Also avoid getting rooked into being the teacher or trainer. This is an inappropriate role for a woman and ultimately counter-productive. As women, we do not really know how a man deconstructs his sexist conditioning: He comes to consciousness as an oppressor; we come to consciousness as the oppressed. The curriculum for re-education is entirely different. Ultimately, to make authentic change, a man must take responsibility for his own education (just as whites must assume responsibility for unlearning racist behavior). A woman may significantly contribute to a man's re-education, however, by modeling self-love, which prohibits him from violating her and contradicts the dominant-subordinate paradigm.

FIELD NOTE

You cannot teach an iceberg how to melt.

🐦 *Can a woman ever trust a man?*

A woman can trust a man to *be* a man. She cannot trust a man to never hurt her. Under male supremacy, a woman's mistrust of men is a healthy and realistic attitude.

FIELD NOTE

The arctic is cold.

🐦 *Under these circumstances, how does one overcome hopelessness?*

By realizing that in accepting the truth of our plight we create the opportunity to address the actual problem. Hopelessness is the herald of pragmatism. While the possibility of safely cultivating female power in heterosexual relationships may be remote, it is through our courageous grasp of the real situation that we find creative and effective ways to progress.

FIELD NOTE

The arctic will always be cold.

☿ *Is separatism the only solution to the predicament of hetero-sexual feminism?*

Well, it is one of the solutions. Separatism is the practice of limiting the oppressor's access to the oppressed, a basic right of self-determination. This practice exists on a continuum. One act of separatism is to require a man to wear a condom during intercourse—you are still very close but there is a boundary.[6] Another is to claim a room of your own with a door that locks. Another is to leave a man who persists in violating you. Another is to walk out of a room where men are verbally demeaning women. I believe the cultivation of female power under male supremacy requires the practice of separatism to a lesser or greater extent, depending on the individual situation. Relief from constant exposure to men and male needs is necessary for a woman to perceive the depth of her innate female power, which she is conditioned to ignore, deny, destroy, or sacrifice. Time spent alone and in consciously constructed women-only space allows a woman to explore aspects of herself that cannot surface in the company of men.

FIELD NOTE

The purpose of a greenhouse is to simulate the tropics. Its seams must be tight. The prevailing winds of the arctic are persistent.

☿ *Aren't you actually saying that to be a real feminist, a woman has to become a lesbian?*

No. I believe a "real" feminist is a woman who loves herself and expresses that love, and who acknowledges the admittedly depressing reality of how the ideology of male supremacy is de-signed to keep her from doing so. Lesbians are not necessarily more feminist than heterosexual women; in fact they may not be feminists at all. As emphasized previously, no one escapes induction into the dominant-subordinate paradigm imposed by male supremacy. Lesbians, too, must work hard to create new ways of being in relationship. Avoiding men does not eliminate internalized oppression or unconscious obedience to oppressive values. However, it is important for heterosexual women to respect the fact that, metaphorically speaking, lesbians definitely log more time in the tropics. Knowing what we know about the hazards of the arctic clime, the positive effects of woman-loving on the cultivation of the orchid of female power cannot be disputed.

FIELD NOTE

To find a warmer climate, move closer to the equator.

Constructing a Greenhouse: Meeting the Needs of Orchids

To grow orchids in the arctic, we must build a greenhouse that will approximate a tropical climate and create a nurturing space while withstanding an aggressively antithetical environment. As an orchid requires rich soil, abundant sunlight and moisture, tropical temperature, structural support, and protection from hostile elements, the blossom of female power has specific and uncompromising needs. An effective greenhouse for the heterosexual feminist might consist of the following:

- ☞ participation in a consciousness-raising group of like-minded women to share experiences and strategies in the arctic;
- ☞ logging regular time in women-only space and spending time alone;
- ☞ practicing conscious acts of separatism and observing your reactions;

🌺 becoming a skilled observer, and avoider, of the dynamics of male supremacy;

🌺 keeping a journal to increase self-awareness;

🌺 working actively in organizations that confront male power abuse and serve women who are harmed by it;

🌺 never tolerating a male companion's violation of your being;

🌺 maintaining a clear perspective and assessment of the pervasive influence of male supremacy and woman-hating on your intimate relationships;

🌺 expecting the men you love and who love you to work actively to make the world safe for women, to be your allies against male power abuse, and to work for gender justice.

When heterosexual feminists deny the risks and dangers inherent in a woman's intimate proximity to men, they consign their female power to the icy tomb of cognitive dissonance—the ability to hold contradictory beliefs in the mind simultaneously without acknowledging the contradiction. Denial only benefits the oppressor. The goal here is to be wise and successful cultivators of our essential female power, wherever we are, whomever our companions of choice. Assess the relative challenge of your chosen situation and devise your strategy accordingly. For the heterosexual feminist, however, hoping for an early spring is not an option.

NOTES

1   Some curious facts about orchids. There are over thirty thousand wild species, and over seventy thousand hybrid species in existence (the

orchid being the apparent object of considerable fetishism in many cultures for eons). While the overwhelming majority of them appear in tropical climates, they actually grow all over the world, including seven varieties that have been found in the arctic. We might commend the peculiar persistence of these orchids. Orchids are half-epiphytes, clinging to the surfaces of other plants for support; but unlike parasites, their roots have no connection with the host plant. The name "orchid" comes from *orchis,* meaning "testicle" because some people, presumably male, found a similarity in shape. The ancient Greek physician Dioscorides used orchids in the treatment of male sexual problems and to help produce male children. I doubt if he was successful.

2   Adrienne Rich, "Compulsory Heterosexuality and Lesbian Existence," in *Blood, Bread, and Poetry: Selected Prose 1979–1985* (New York: W. W. Norton, 1986), 51. Many of the fundamental ideas mentioned in this essay are articulated fully in this important work.

3   Sarah Lucia Hoagland, *Lesbian Ethics: Toward New Value* (Palo Alto, CA: Institute of Lesbian Studies, 1988), 29. Hoagland's analysis of heterosexualism is brilliant.

4   For a definitive treatment of this concept, see Andrea Dworkin, *Intercourse* (New York: Macmillan, 1987). The following three quotes are shockingly pertinent:

"The political meaning of intercourse for women is the fundamental question of feminism and freedom: can an occupied people—physically occupied inside, internally invaded—be free; can those with a metaphysically compromised privacy have self-determination; can those without a biologically based physical integrity have self-respect?" (123).

"Intercourse occurs in a context of a power relation that is pervasive and incontrovertible. The context in which the act takes place, whatever the meaning of the act in and of itself, is one in which men have social, economic, political, and physical power over women. Some men do not have all those kinds of power over all women; but all men have some kinds of power over all women; and most men have controlling power over what they call *their* women—the women they fuck. The power is predetermined by gender, by being male" (126).

"How to separate the act of intercourse from the social reality of male power is not clear, especially because it is male power that constructs both the meaning and the current practice of intercourse as such" (127).

5   Charlie Kreiner, "About Men: A Conversation with Charlie Kreiner," *The Breitenbush Newsletter,* Winter–Spring 1990, 23. Kreiner is a practitioner of re-evaluation counseling who currently specializes in men's conditioning. I suspect he would take issue with my analysis.

6   Unless, of course, you are trying to get pregnant. If not, even if the woman uses birth control, using a condom reminds the man that he is responsible for his own body; here, its roles in conception and contagion.

Responses

As an editor trying to publish "feminist" (a word I didn't use) work at a mainstream publishing house (i.e., a hostile environment, for the most part), I have had wonderful opportunities, again, to observe the workings of what your readers understand as patriarchal conditions (and that others simply don't think about at all—*patriarchal* is not a word in common use) at work.

Publishing is an interesting place—where meanings are created and exploited. Some books try to help people make sense of their lives; others try to "force" a sense on people's lives that readers accept (creating financial gain for the publisher and a salary for the editor) or reject (causing the reverse). Some years ago, I signed up Andrea Dworkin's *Letters from a War Zone* and so had occasion to present—to colleagues, salespeople, etc.— radical feminism as something that readers would "accept." As you might guess, this was not easy. At lunch one day, I was having a conversation with one of my colleagues about rape. I suggested that she might be interested in Andrea's book and offered to get her a copy (then in manuscript form). She paused. "No," she said, "I just can't read that. I'm enough of a man-hater as it is. And look where it's gotten me!" (i.e., critical of most men and past partners; currently single and "looking"). "I can't let myself get any angrier. I can't read any further." She is in a state that many women are in, and I was grateful that she'd been honest enough to say more than just "No, thank you," the usual response of women when offered the opportunity to become more intimate with feminist thought in general and Dworkin's work in particular.

Unfortunately the benefits of having a feminist conscious-ness are not all that evident to most women. It's a state of mind to be detoured around, one that will take them even farther from where they want to be: in a loving, close, "good" relation-ship with a man. "We" know that's not necessarily true, and all the reasons why, but "we" haven't done a very good job, re-cently, of putting it into words. As feminists, we must find new and better ways to talk about the positives, the payoffs, of our "raised" consciousness; not just the problems we constantly run into on a daily basis in P.C. (patriarchal culture!). Or else . . . the arctic is going to stay, for the most part, deflowered.

Carole J. DeSanti, New York, NY

First I began thinking about tomatoes (à la orchids) and the fact that hothouse varieties do not have the taste and beauty of the naturally grown variety. . . . I think it is very difficult for women to move toward increasing self-love and empowerment while in a greenhouse, even though it protects them from the arctic of heterosexual relationships. It takes energy to maintain the pro-tected environment—energy that detracts from growth (energy resources aren't infinite!). Furthermore it is hard to get the greenhouse climate just right. While you are confined you also aren't free to move about and seek those places that would pro-mote your growth. In other words, a greenhouse is an artificial environment.

I sincerely question whether a woman can reach her full fem-inist potential in a heterosexual partnership (though I do think being heterosexual and not married may be somewhat different from being heterosexual and married). Escaping—partially or totally—a heterosexual partnership isn't enough, but it is necessary for growth toward self-love (either get into the greenhouse or get to a place where the greenhouse isn't necessary). I tend to think right now that the more you escape oppressive institutions, the better your potential for becoming a self-loving woman. Since "feminist" isn't a dichotomous notion (there are qualitative differences among feminists), I have no trouble with heterosexuality coexisting with feminism. But I do think there are places of self-love that heterosexual feminists just can't reach because they have to spend time in greenhouses in a hostile climate.

Also, returning to the tomato analogy, there is some difference between hothouse and homegrown tomatoes. Eating hothouse tomatoes reminds me of what can be. I suspect my analogy is breaking down here, because I really do not want to view heterosexual feminists as "worse" than lesbian feminists in the self-love and oppression-resisting categories, and I really don't think they are. It's just that they are different, and awareness of those differences has potential for moving us all to a greater ability to live as self-loving women.

Thinking back on my own experience as a once-married, heterosexual feminist (and now a lesbian feminist), I found I had to leave the arctic greenhouse and move into an environment less fundamentally hostile to my feminism. As the political reality of my oppression became clearer to me (and I was in a marriage that even by many feminist standards would have been considered excellent), I saw oppression everywhere. When I saw it in places that I could do something about (like my marriage, which I could terminate) I had to do it. The arctic greenhouse helped me to nurture enough self-love to see where I had to go. In that sense the greenhouse experience was a good one. It gave me a sense of direction about what I needed to change.

We all have to construct artificial environments to help us deal with patriarchy. I need a greenhouse to shelter me from the academic (academented) environment where I earn a living. Yet the oppression I feel in academia does not seem so pervasive and fundamental as the oppression of marriage. They are quite different in ways I haven't quite sorted out.

Thanks for this essay. Now I must tell you—I don't really like tomatoes!

Maeona K. Kramer, Sandy, UT

I differ with you on the question of "exceptional" men. I do not believe it is simply denial to believe "some men are different." Some men simply haven't been socialized properly to play their role as dominators, or circumstances have forced them to acquire very different traits. I know a man, for example, the eldest of four, whose parents were killed in a plane crash when he was a teenager. As a result he was forced into a nurturing role and has had many of the same experiences and problems women have—he gave up his career until late in life in order to care for others; he naturally thinks of others before himself; kids are drawn to him.

On the other hand, take me. As an only child, I, like many other only children, was not as thoroughly socialized to my gender role as those around me. In the famous Carol Gilligan/Rohlberg experiment where women don't give firm answers to the question, Should the man steal the drug for his sick wife?, I was always in the steal-the-drug category. Women hurt other women all the time, yet I know at least one man who has not hurt another in eighteen years. That doesn't mean of course that these men don't slip occasionally into the privilege of the dominant culture. But their basic temperament is of a very different order. I know one man who sees sexist relationships around him more easily than half the women I know, including myself.

Yet your essay raises a more complex issue. Is it really wonderful to live in a state of constant pain, as one would if one thought like you? If you really believe men will always hurt you, I can't see any alternative but separatism. Masochism is not a solution. Women are stronger than that, really! They actually often have loving relationships with women and with men, where they are not in constant pain. We've been given this B.S. about "working at relationships." I've been in a relationship for fifteen years, and in that time have had maybe eight or nine intense arguments. For us, the world is where you fight. Home is the safe harbor. That this relationship happens to be with a man I regard as a fluke, since previously I was involved with women. Incidentally, I have always been the main wage-earner and in many ways the more powerful, though not necessarily the smarter or more psychic one. So I've thrown all categories out the window.

Margot Adler, New York, NY

You've hit the nail right on the head. I am appalled at the escalating violence against women. Several, just in northern Wisconsin, have been killed the last couple of years for trying to leave a relationship. This society, as it is now, provides no protection for women. They are always at the mercy of the stronger sex, and more and more men are proving to have no mercy at all. I appreciate your list of things to do—they seem clear, concise, and possible!

As I grow older, I value more and more the closeness and sharing of communities of women. We should teach all of our daughters to look for and form these relationships for the strength they give.

E. M., Wheeler, WI

The Invisible Obvious

Unnatural but familiar
the fear eases on
with the smooth wrapping
of a shroud.
I feel them heavy-handed
on my shoulders:
The politics of self-betrayal,
the autorape of submission.
I pledge to break free.
There are no rules for war.
My fight begins and ends inside,
without indication to others.
No faults.
No excuses.[1]

Soon after writing this poem in 1978, I began an experiment in my journal. I wrote each morning with a new commitment: To write down all the voices I could hear inside my head, to censor nothing. Over a year's time, I discovered many intriguing things about myself and my internal "committee," but by far the most disturbing was what I learned about my conditioning. The interplay among the many inner voices, and my external responses to them, indicated clearly that I was programmed to self-destruct.

I do not mean that I was suicidal, or that I lived recklessly, like someone who might be called a thrill seeker, someone who lives on the edge. Quite the contrary. I was responsible to a fault. I saw myself as Little Miss Perfect: self-righteous, ultracorrect, and fastidiously martyred. But what I noticed in the patterns revealed by my uncensored journal was that at the core of my self-regard was hatred. I sabotaged my earnest efforts and ridiculed my accomplishments. I doubted my abilities and anticipated failure. Underneath my perfectionism and superiority, I appeared to despise myself.

This realization rocked my careful house-of-cards life like an earthquake. Not only was I ashamed and shocked, but I was entirely uncertain about what my life would be like without that self-hatred. My journal showed me it was the subtle underpinning that shored up my every belief and perspective. Without it, what would hold my life together? This was the beginning of my understanding of internalized oppression.

The task: How to control a group of human beings who slightly outnumber you and your group. You want them to be obedient, hardworking, energetic, loyal, and loving upon command, as a group and as individuals. You want them to defer to your wishes, and enjoy it. You want them to train their children to do the same. You are willing to use force, even violence, but you would prefer something more subtle, less time-consuming and costly. You have more important things to do.

> *Oppression is a system of interrelated barriers and forces which reduce, immobilize and mold people who belong to a certain group, and effect their subordination to another group.*
>
> Marilyn Frye[2]

When viewed dispassionately, without moral judgment, the phenomenon of male dominance is striking. The sheer mechanics are mind-boggling. How is it that a minority of human beings of one gender maintains control over the others, in virtually every culture and corner of the planet? Clearly this feat could not be accomplished without the apparent cooperation of those controlled.

When women first become aware of oppression, we usually do not look to the culture for causes, we look to blame ourselves, as if we simply voted for the wrong candidate or fell in love with the wrong guy. As if patriarchy began a few years ago, with Reagan or Nixon. Or Roosevelt or Truman. Or Hitler, Stalin, Pope Gregory, or Thomas Aquinas or Aristotle. But the practice of domination was first recorded over five thousand years ago, far beyond our personal control. Many researchers have suggested that this practice began when men subordinated women to control their fertility, to claim ownership of their children.[3] This is why the term *patriarchy* seems appropriate to describe the politics of domination: the rule of the fathers. Apparently the disruption of a long-standing culture of harmony, equality, and natural interdependence began when men first used force to control women. Over thousands of years, this principle has become woven into the fabric of society, expanding to the proportions it has reached today, manifested in complex, pervasive, institutionalized systems of oppression and extending far beyond male supremacy. In this lifetime, a culture of domination is all we have ever known.

You cannot understand the mysterious love that hurts you.
It comes, slowly at first, building, until you are surrounded
with what you feel as warmth, what you know as peace until
you raise your arms high in surrender
for you want every part of you warmed, eased,
and the love you know puts a hot hand over your mouth,
a forearm around your neck, you are powerless to stop it
from enclosing you.
The mystery of the love that holds you hostage.

For subordination to be permanent and cost effective, it is necessary to create conditions such that the subordinated group acquiesces to some extent in the subordination. Probably one of the most efficient ways to secure acquiescence is to convince the people that their subordination is inevitable.

Marilyn Frye[4]

As Marilyn Frye has elegantly described, the task of oppressing humans poses challenges absent in the oppression of other creatures, for "this one matches the exploiter in intelligence and fineness of physical abilities, and this one is capable of self-respect, righteousness and resentment."[5] In order to establish and maintain efficient dominance, Frye suggests, the subordinates (who presumably would not elect a status of inferiority) must be convinced that their subordination is inevitable, even natural. Such internalized oppression creates the illusion of agreement. If we are obedient of our own will (albeit a manipulated one), the patriarchy does not have to restrict us with physical bonds or incarceration. Those kinds of restrictions are labor-intensive, expensive, and create public-relations problems for the dominators. Altering individual consciousness to support patriarchal values is a much more attractive alternative in that it is cost-effective, convenient, and as a form of control, it is virtually invisible. Susan Faludi observes a case in point: "A backlash against women's rights succeeds to the degree that it appears not to be political, that it appears not to be a struggle at all. It is most powerful when it goes private, when it lodges inside a woman's mind and turns her vision inward, until she imagines the pressure is all in her head, until she begins to enforce the backlash, too—on herself."[6] Thus, internalized oppression is a primary tool for maintaining abusive hierarchy in all its aspects: sexism, racism, homophobia, ableism, classism, ageism, heterosexualism, and so on.

But as a form of social control, internalization is definitely a long-range strategy. This method requires that over many generations, the values of domination must be passed down through family and other societal forms. Our conditioning from birth trains us to conform and to assume those values as our own. Given no alternatives, domination and subordination becomes our reality, our universe. It's just the way things are.

Although this tool is used to maintain dominance over any number of groups and individuals, in this essay I am most

interested in scrutinizing the role of internalization in the per-
petuation of sexism, of male dominance. In other cases of dominance—white supremacy, for example, or class hierarchies—
the controlled group generally rumbles with discontent and
seizes opportunities for liberation. But women in general (at
least in the versions of history we are told) have rebelled only
rarely, in small numbers, unsuccessfully. This is not to dismiss
the valiant continuing efforts of thousands of women over centuries (including myself and probably most readers of this essay),
yet male domination remains.

I'm oversimplifying, of course, but I am perplexed by this particular characteristic of women's subordination: Ask a woman in
the United States if she is oppressed as a woman, and she will
probably say no. Then she will return to her word processor in
the typing pool where she earns seventy cents to the male dollar,
or to her split-level in the suburbs where she cares for the home
and children of a man who beats her, or she will resume her therapy session where she is trying to decipher fragmented memories of incest, or she'll continue stuffing envelopes for the
campaign to fight toxic waste in her drinking water then walk
home past the park where a man raped her last year.[7] Women
may be the only oppressed group in the world who, by and large,
have difficulty recognizing our own oppression.

Recent U.S. Justice Department statistics show that twenty-
one thousand violent male assaults on women are reported
every week. Despite such overwhelming and insidious evidence
of woman-hating (not to mention economic and legal in-
equities), we consistently deny the connections between our
daily experiences and the institution of male supremacy. To me,
this indicates the extent of our psychic and psychological colo-

nization, as well as the phenomenal effectiveness of internalized oppression. We are not consciously aware of making a choice to follow patriarchal values, but we do—of our own volition—choose them. We are not aware of other options, and we are not aware of our own volition. These are symptoms of what Mary Daly calls the Robot: automatic, unquestioned obedience.

At the same time, it should be noted that our consensus denial reveals the dominator's weakest point. Consciousness is the subordinate's threshold to power, guarded only by an act of will. We can choose to internalize anything.

> *At the bell,*
> *you have begun.*
> *Defer to the man on your left.*
> *He has some answers. Move away.*
> *You feel graceless, awkward as a fawn.*
> *When you turn from the window,*
> *you find a different room.*
> *The trees around the lake are familiar.*
> *You reach for the door.*

Many of our internal voices suggest oppressive values, such as "Men are more important than women," "White people are superior to black people," "Control of emotion is better than expression of emotion." As women under male supremacy, the conditioning we have internalized might tell us, among other things, "Your body is imperfect," "You are unable to take care of yourself," "You need male approval for validation," "You are an object, not a person," "It is impolite to feel or show anger." Our inner voices echo the woman-hating at the core of society as we personally customize the general cues of the patriarchy. This is a disturbing realization, for it means that in each moment our own internal voices direct us to act in small ways that, cumulatively, serve to oppress us. In this direct, immediate, and intimate way, we unwittingly reinforce our own oppression.

What can we do about this? Since the voices are our own, we can change them. By increasing our awareness of our conditioning and of the possibilities beyond it, we can change the way we live our daily lives. We can learn to tell the difference between what is essential and what is imposed. We can learn to discern the many options available and decide to replace the patriarchal beliefs inside us with those of our own choosing, those that reflect and support values that are in harmony with our current, evolving desires and visions.

To do this we must learn to identify the basic frame of reference implanted by the dominator's conditioning. We must examine our basic orientation and reconsider it—attitude by attitude, decision by decision, choice by choice, moment by moment. This is a process, a skill, a way of being, not a sudden religious conversion after which we are instantly transformed. Developing the ability to see beyond the paradigm of patriarchy, and to break the hold of internalized oppression, is a matter of intention, will, and growing consciousness. As Virginia Woolf suggested, since we are not accustomed to it, women must "practice the habit of freedom."

> *I myself have never been able to find out precisely what feminism is: I only know that people call me a feminist whenever I express sentiments that differentiate me from a doormat or a prostitute.*
>
> Rebecca West, 1913

I'm sure it's no coincidence that my intensified desire for self-awareness and my introduction to feminism occurred during the same period. Beginning with Marilyn French's novel *The Women's Room,* proceeding to Susan Griffin's *Woman and Nature,* working up my courage to read Mary Daly's *Beyond God the Father* and *Gyn/Ecology,* I read my way into a sturdy new life, one that is not a house of cards. Feminism offers a worldview that includes me, not as a doormat, but as an intelligent participant, capable of dramatically influencing the quality of my own life and, in doing so, the world around me. Feminism suggests that by loving myself, I will change the world. At first this seemed unacceptably selfish to me. But I have decided to risk it.

Feminism's analysis of world culture points out what I call the invisible obvious. We live in a society that is male-supremacist and misogynist. Our "civilization" allows and encourages the hatred of women. Not just men hating women, but women hating women and me hating myself. But the house of cards that is patriarchy depends on our unconscious, automatic self-hatred for its stability. Without our cooperation, the oppressive system fails—immediately on many intimate levels, and gradually, I believe, on all levels.

In an essential way, then, this seemingly seamless culture of dominance is held together by our individual belief in the lie of self-hatred. This is not to blame the victims. This is to notice the point of power we hold in each moment, to cooperate or resist. To accept self-hate or choose self-love. This is to crack the code of our conditioning, to release our intelligence and creativity from internalized oppression into harmony with our healing and growth. This is to recognize that the patriarchy is not the universe. We are.

Beyond all hope, you look into a mirror
to find yourself, and you do:
reflected, perfect, shimmering
back and forth on the light, dancing
on the water, gliding
into the eyes of the reflection.
She looks at your face. You smile.
Everything is quiet. She touches
you without words, and her touch sings
over your skin like the water
and you dance to no music but her eyes.
When you embrace, the water is cool.
Under the surface, you make plans.

NOTES

1   All poems written in 1978–79 by Kay Leigh Hagan.

2   Marilyn Frye, "Sexism," in *The Politics of Reality: Essays in Feminist Theory* (Freedom, CA: Crossing Press, 1983), 33.

3   See the works of Gerda Lerner, Marija Gimbutas, Riane Eisler, Monica Sjöö, and Barbara Mor, listed in Related Resources.

4   Marilyn Frye, "In and out of Harm's Way: On Arrogance and Love," in *The Politics of Reality*, 59.

5   Ibid.

6   Susan Faludi, *Backlash: The Undeclared War on American Women* (New York: Crown, 1991), xxii.

7   I have deliberately chosen experiences of middle-class women. Because we have more discernible choices than women from working or poverty classes, our complacency exemplifies most vividly the power of internalized oppression.

Responses

I was active politically in the women's movement in the late 1970s and early 1980s and am most recently again in the pro-choice movement. Your statement, "Despite the overwhelming and insidious evidence of woman-hating, we consistently deny the connections between our daily experiences and the institution of male supremacy" struck me. I'm sixty years old, and I can understand and appreciate why my Italian-born, uneducated mother would sigh woefully and say, "It's a man's world." I didn't understand at the time what she meant, but I knew she was captive in an abusive relationship.

That was a very long time ago. Things have changed so much, and yet I keep wondering how the majority of women in this country could have voted for Ronald Reagan and George Bush! Your essay has helped to put it, once again, in proper perspective. The fears women revealed concerning the changes proposed by the Equal Rights Amendment, and the role women are playing in the so-called pro-life movement, are harsh examples of our need to perpetuate our own oppression.

Kay Wiley, San Francisco, CA

I am convinced that as the walls of Berlin, the Warsaw Pact, and the Kremlin have fallen, so vast changes are occurring inside myself. The walls inside me are falling. It takes hundreds of women as examples. It takes thousands of individual steps. It takes re-creating daily a pact with myself that I belong here, right here on this planet. The intent, the spirit that I take into each day, is the measure of success in my life. The wake of hundreds of thousands of others who dare to do the same thing is what reminds me. The voyage is a solitary one, but many make the journey at the same time.

Amy Estelle, Keene, NH

I believe that every seemingly tiny infraction of one of the rules of patriarchy is a significant step toward ending the oppression of women. At first I thought that breaking a rule only in my thoughts was taking only the tiniest of baby steps. But the opposite is true, because patriarchal control of our thoughts is its most powerful tool. It is imperative that we vigorously and aggressively assert control over our own thoughts by breaking the rule of hatred of ourselves. We must each commit to loving our precious self unconditionally. This is done through daily affirmations and by becoming aware of every self-criticizing thought that crosses our minds:

> When we trip and stumble, we can affirm how precious we are in our distraction.

> When we are inarticulate, we can affirm how precious we are in our excitement.

> When we are forgetful, we can affirm how precious we are in our preoccupation.

> When we make a mistake, we can affirm how perfectly imperfect we are and love ourselves for it.

The day these thoughts begin to occur spontaneously is a glorious triumph. The ripple effect this way of thinking will have on our lives is certain to be vast.

Sue Gibson, Dallas, TX

Heart Sisters:

Loving Each Other Over Time

*How do women live in the world as men have
defined it while creating the world as women
imagine it could be?*

Janice Raymond[1]

One Thursday night around 1944 in a small town in North Carolina, nine women gathered. Their purpose: to play cards. And play they did. Nearly fifty years later, they're still at it, the Thursday Bridge Club, alternate Thursdays, without fail. My mother was one of the original members of the group, and the women of the Thursday Bridge Club have been "other mothers" to me from the day I was born. I have benefited from this relationship in uncountable ways, not the least of which is their living model of enduring love among women.

What I want to explore here is that most precious experience: Women loving each other over time, through change, despite oppression, and with joy. The Bridge Club is, for me, a symbol of this love, arising from my own heritage. At the risk of idealizing a few middle-class white women playing cards, I find in the Bridge Club lessons in woman-loving, some so practical as to be painful, others so obvious they are easily missed. What I share with you here is part memoir, part fantasy, and part longing for a Bridge Club of my own.

From the stories my mother tells of her girlhood, she was a bit of a wild one. Headstrong, opinionated, indulged as much as an only child could be during the Depression, the daughter of two teenaged runaways from Sandy Ridge, North Carolina, a rural community of tobacco farmers, Mary Ferguson grew up in the bustling town of Winston-Salem, where the main products were textiles and cigarettes. When she was sixteen, the same year she met my father on a blind date, her father bought her a car—a Buick, she was proud to tell me—undoubtedly making her the envy of her friends in 1938. She was pretty and smart, finishing high school and two years of business school, doing secretarial work before landing a job as a reservationist for Eastern Airlines. She tells many stories of trips she took, flying free as an employee, and how she was the first woman in North Carolina to get a pilot's license. My father, a dark-haired zoot-suited dandy from neighboring Greensboro and seven years her senior, wooed this independent, strong-minded young woman unsuccessfully for several years. On his B-52 he painted "Wait For Me, Mary," had a buddy take a snapshot, sent it to her from overseas. Finally she agreed to marry him on a furlough from the air force. She was twenty-two years old. The year was 1944.

I tell you all this because context is important. I've never asked my mom what she felt like when she was flying or how she felt about giving it up, but the contrasting images of aviatrix and suburban housewife convey in a nutshell the about-face women were dealt by society in those crucial years coming out of World War II. Rosie the Riveter to Betty Crocker. Get out of the work force please, girls; we need those jobs for the returning G.I.'s, and in exchange we have for each of you a box in the 'burbs. My mother talks of the hard-sell pitches for domestic bliss splashed all over the women's magazines. "Like propaganda," she remarks. "How You Can Support Our Boys" by creating a happy, happy home for them to return to. On Magnolia Street she set up house, had a baby, then had another. Most of her friends were doing the same. Amid the sweet challenges of child rearing, she remembers isolation, boredom, and claustrophobia from those years. Her flying days were over.

It was right about this time that the Bridge Club began. I don't know whose idea it was, but it was a good one. Mary, Lois, Dotty, Martha, the two Libs, Pokey, Jerri, and Mildred had been friends since high school or met behind baby strollers in their new neighborhood. Some of my earliest memories are of pleading with my mother to let me stay up "until the Bridge Club gets here." They rotated houses on a biweekly basis, and the Thursdays the Bridge Club met at our house seemed few, far between, and extremely exciting to me. By this time they had been going for a good six or seven years, and the basic ritual was set: Gather at 8:00 P.M., chat through dessert, then play two rubbers of bridge. Hostess poured coffee and kept up a running commentary on the game. Generally husbands disappeared voluntarily, for the combined energy of nine women set to have fun proved far too intimidating. Children could stay through dessert, but when the cards came out, only the women remained. I remember drifting to sleep lulled by their laughter, feeling that something special was happening in our house that night.

Perhaps you are getting impatient with my tale of ordinary women doing ordinary things. I told you this loving was practical, so practical perhaps as to be dull. Let me explain what I find of interest here.

I tend to think that playing bridge was an innocuous cover for a support system of women isolated from one another by the rigors of social and political propriety in 1950s America and the single-minded focus required of Spockian motherhood. In addition to their biweekly card games, the Bridge Club women shared resources, wisdom, and even magic, creating a space to celebrate and empower themselves within a sanitized misogyny desperately reinventing itself.

I'm sure they will laugh when they read this! Their potlucks, seasonal swaps of children's clothing, annual group beach vacations, and baby-sitting trades may hardly seem the stuff of liberation, much less revolution. Yet as I study the patterns of male domination, and the subtle thoroughness of our five-millennium oppression, I have come to believe that whenever women gather to talk about our lives, to share resources, and to make merry, we claim ourselves. We create a culture we were never intended to have. Marilyn French has said, "Pleasure enlarges the spirit and, like power, it is contagious."[2] Sometimes I try to imagine what my mother's life would have been like without the Bridge Club, but the thought is too grim to hold for long.

It was a means of survival, the Bridge Club; literally a "living beyond" the confining aspects of motherhood, martyrdom, and marriage. It was a women-only space, claimed for the purpose of having fun, a biweekly minifestival, if you will, circa 1950. But there was another level to the sharing of these women. They were Heart Sisters.

The ritual of Heart Sisters took place at the Bridge Club's annual December holiday luncheon, which also rotated. Since one had to host it only once a decade, members expected and received an elegant meal, the menu of which was always of great interest to me. Afterward names were drawn by secret lot to determine Heart Sisters for the coming year. The results were absolutely sacred, revealed only at the next year's luncheon. The mission of your Heart Sister, as far as I have been able to determine, was solely to surprise and delight you.

They were devoted to giving pleasure, acknowledging accomplishments, surprising each other anonymously and often. Once on my mother's birthday, for instance, I remember opening the front door to check the early morning weather as I prepared for school. There on the step was a basket full of little gifts, topped with a bow and a card. I carried it in to the breakfast table and watched Mom's face spread into a slow smile as she read the inscription. "My Heart Sister," she said, taking the basket into her room. I understood these gestures to be a private sort of thing, although occasionally I was pressed into service in the name of preserving the sacred secrets. When preparing Mildred's anniversary present one year, Mom asked me to letter the card. "We passed notes to each other in high school," she said in exasperation. "She'd recognize my writing in a second." Then I was enlisted to skulk through the neighborhood to make the delivery as she waited two blocks away. "And don't get caught!" she warned as I started my dash through the shrubbery.

Heart Sisters would sometimes go to great lengths to outdo and fool one another, sneaking bottles of champagne into refrigerators as laundry was being shifted from washer to dryer or mailing gifts from distant cities to avoid discovery. I think of the Heart Sisters as a ritual of endearment, affection, and delight. The Heart Sisters worked a kind of practical magic on each other. This circle of support included not only tools for survival but also felicity, playfulness, and joy. These elements are essential in our daily lives, for they create, if only momentarily, an alternative, an experience of a loving world, a society of mutual respect and affirmation.

The first year I attended the Michigan Womyn's Music Festival, I was walking through the lush, fern-filled woods when I encountered a banner tied high between two trees. White with lettering of silver glitter, the banner read, simply, "Celebrate Womyn." I was stunned and suddenly tearful, imagining what the world might be like if the messages surrounding us at every turn of the dial, page, and corner exhorted us to "Celebrate Womyn" instead of, say, "Drink Coke for Breakfast." In that moment of insight, I pledged to celebrate womyn at every opportunity, in ways communicating that message to myself as well as others. This is, I think, the revolutionary aspect of the Heart Sisters, whose purpose, it could be said, was to celebrate womyn.

The Bridge Club, as noted previously, is an ongoing venture, complete with biweekly games and ancillary activities. They celebrated fifty years of friendship last summer at a gathering that included dozens of children and grandchildren, the Grand Slam, they dubbed it. During our last visit, Mom told me that Martha had sprained her ankle. The Bridge Club was taking meals over, she said, adding that Martha's husband, a victim of Alzheimer's, was "like a child now." The nature of support has changed as their needs have changed, and I envy their continuity. "Someone to grow old with" times nine. Women loving each other over time.

But times have changed. My mother's Bridge Club, like the quilting bee before it, is the product of another era, and I suspect it would not work for me today, although I am a recent convert to the wisdom of a biweekly game of cards. I search for my own circle of loving women, and I find them all over the country, scattered outposts of affirmation in a vast misogyny constantly reinventing itself, even now. Though work that demands frequent travel has made the steady presence of a Bridge Club impossible for me (and, after all, at my age they were well into their second decade!), I proudly claim my long-term women friends as Heart Sisters—a tribute to the years of enduring love still being shared by my mother and her circle.

Not every woman friend is a Heart Sister to me. They are precious and distinctive, proving themselves over time and trial. For me, it is the loving through change that distinguishes the Heart Sister. In her constancy and acceptance, she creates a space in me for trust that I am loved. She is a reliable mirror for my reality, sometimes validating my perceptions, often astonishing me with insights I have missed. She is honest, direct, and gentle. She makes a ritual out of celebrating the simple fact of my being, reflecting back to me the need to appreciate myself, to love my self. Joy is the watchword of the Heart Sister.

"There is no final end," says Marilyn French, "there is only the doing well, being what we want to be, doing what we want to do, living in delight." My Heart Sisters remind me of this essential truth by modeling courage, imagination, and creativity. It is in the mundane setting of our daily lives that we

exert our greatest influence. Despite the elaborate and desper-
ate attempts of the dominant culture to distract us, the enduring
love among women, expressed in the most ordinary of ways,
guides our attention again and again to the power at our core.
". . . It is possible to live with an eye to delight rather than to
domination. And this is the feminist morality," says French.

Loving over time, respecting change, mirroring our realities,
unfailing honesty, the sharing of resources, creating a personal
culture to celebrate ourselves as women—this is what I offer my
Heart Sisters and what I have come to expect of them. This is
what was modeled for me by those who came before. What I am
suggesting here is that we acknowledge the immediate transfor-
mative energy of our commitments to one another. That we
practice rituals of endearment, affection, and delight with the
same earnestness we use to challenge abuse of power. That we
appreciate the extraordinary influence of a thoughtful gesture.
That we understand the revolutionary significance of women's
enduring love for women, wherever it can be found and in whatever form.

Now. Whose turn is it to deal?

NOTES

(My thanks to the Heart Sisters who convened at Labrys Wilderness
Retreat for women in Honor, Michigan, over Oestre 1991, for your questions, scrutiny, and scarf dances.)

1   Janice Raymond, *A Passion for Friends: Toward a Philosophy of
Female Affection* (Boston: Beacon Press, 1986), 205.

2   This and all subsequent quotes are from Marilyn French, *Beyond
Power: On Women, Men, and Morals* (New York: Simon & Schuster,
1985).

Responses

Thanks to our mothers and foremothers for their bridge clubs, sewing circles, and quilting bees. They kept something alive for us, something we now can take further than they were able to because of their isolation and unnamed oppression.

Four years ago I began meeting with a support group of women. We don't play bridge, though occasionally we get together for slumber parties or weekends at the beach or in the mountains. Our regular meetings, though, consist of brief updates about our lives since we last met, sharing something "new and good" to remind ourselves that no matter what is hard in our lives, we can find something joyful or courageous, and then dividing the remaining time among us, so that each of us has between fifteen and thirty minutes of time in which to talk of whatever troubles us, and the others listen well.

After meeting regularly with this group for about two years, I began to notice a change in myself. Self-doubt and depression gave way to confidence and hopefulness. Every two weeks five women would tell me with words or smiles or touch that I was important to them, important to the world. I began to believe it. I became bolder, took more risks. I know I am loved, no matter what. Old feelings of desperation around relationships have been replaced with the ability to know what I want and the belief that I can get it. I made the leap out of an unsatisfactory career of eighteen years into the adventure of creating meaningful work.

As I have observed myself over these four years, I see that I am internalizing the support and appreciation of the group. As each of us has come up against our fears, hurts, and places of rigid thinking, we have had five other women thinking clearly about us, reminding us of who we really are, and how insignificant our limitations are compared to our abilities.

Many women today have similar support systems and networks that take us a giant step beyond where our mothers could go with their bridge clubs. I don't think they could see out of their internalized oppression the way we can. Their almost underground continuation of the essential elements of support, sharing resources, and having fun has opened the door for us to go farther. While operating under sadly similar oppression, we are creatively moving beyond its influence, thanks to our own heart sisters.

Judith Harriss, Sopchoppy, FL

In my research I came across these quotes, which I couldn't resist sending along; these two women were Heart Sisters indeed!

"So entirely one are we [Susan B. Anthony and Elizabeth Cady Stanton] that in all our associations, ever side by side on the same platform, not one feeling of jealousy or envy has ever shadowed our lives. We have indulged freely in criticism of each other when alone, and hotly contended whenever we have differed, but in our friendship of thirty years there has never been a break of one hour" (Elizabeth Cady Stanton, 1881).

"We have jogged along pretty well for forty years or more. Perhaps mid the wreck of thrones and the undoing of so many friendships, sects, parties and families, you and I deserve some credit for sticking together through all adverse winds, with so few ripples on the surface. . . . Tell our suffrage daughters to brace up and get ready for a long pull, a strong pull, and a pull all together when I come back" (Elizabeth Cady Stanton to Susan B. Anthony, 1887).

"Never expect to know any joy in this world equal to that of going up and down the land, getting good editorials written, engaging halls and circulating Mrs. Stanton's speeches. If I ever have had any inspiration, she has given it to me, for never could I have done my work if I had not had this woman at my right hand" (Susan B. Anthony, remarks at her seventieth birthday celebration, 1890).

Anne Lundquist, Sedalia, NC

Heart Sisters wonderfully illustrates that simple pleasures are the best. I don't play cards, but I enjoy sitting around the table, coffee pot in close vicinity, with a favorite friend or going to the fabric store and planning craft projects with my mom and sister. To the untrained heart these activities don't appear to be of much substance, but they are a great source of joy to me. All women experience the love and magic experienced by your mother and her heart sisters. Thanks!

Paula J. King, Connersville, IN

When I received the essay on Heart Sisters, it took about three weeks for me to get all the way through it. My mother had a bridge club, too. It was her one night a month to get away to be with other women. I think about what a restricted life she led, that she only had one night a month to be a woman and have female connections and bonds and friendship and support. I cried and cried for her.

My father was very dictatorial, manipulative, punitive toward her and all of her children. She divorced him after fourteen years of marriage (thank Goddess) and then started to find herself. She married at sixteen (unwanted pregnancy) and then had three more children by the age of twenty-one. The bridge club was part of her life when I was three to five years old. My father took the opportunity of her absence to terrorize and sexually abuse me. So that even in her single act of taking care of herself, he was raping her, through me.

Every time I picked up "Heart Sisters" to read, I'd start from the beginning and read until I started crying and couldn't read anymore. I wanted to tell you about this in person (this summer at your workshop at the Michigan festival). In fact, sitting in the workshop, I wanted to stand up and tell everyone. Sometimes it's so hard to get my voice. I wondered, as I sat under the tree surrounded by womyn, if anyone else was remembering a similar story.

Today, as I create my own life, I know that each bold step I take is for all womonkind. I know this. I know because I feel the urgings of many womonsouls when I live boldly, and I hear the celebration when I live true to the heart. I know that each time one of us offers our authentic self, it heals all of us.

I am starting a heart sisters circle in my healing-from-incest support group. We have constant membership for ten-week sessions, and then sometimes it changes, so we'll be exchanging heart sisters every ten weeks.

Name withheld on request

Bitches from Hell:

The Politics of Self-Defense

I am answering a survey concerning women's experiences of male violence. Pencil in hand, ready to begin, I feel I am one of the lucky ones.

The statistics are familiar: every fifteen seconds, a woman is beaten; one of four women will be a victim of rape; four out of five murdered women are killed by men—between a half and a third are married to their murderers; 42 percent of all women employed by the federal government, a group the size of Denver, Colorado, have been sexually harassed.

I think I am lucky because only my father has hit me, no stranger-to-stranger rape, only dimly recalled incest, maybe a couple of date rapes, and many times I didn't want to but did it anyway. I've been followed, I had a persistent obscene caller for two years, I've seen numerous men jerking off in cars or in parks, and when I was twenty-five, an employer encouraged me to get drunk, then had sex with me. I've seen and heard men beating women, including my father and mother, and I've intervened in a few public incidents. But all in all, I consider myself lucky. So far, so good.

Do you feel at risk:

in an elevator with a strange man?

parking in a deserted lot?

climbing a stairwell?

hiking or biking alone?

staying alone in a motel?

taking public transportation alone?[1]

As far as I can tell, men's violence against women is part of the invisible obvious of everyday life. Invisible because it is accepted, for the most part goes unpunished, and is rarely even referred to in public or private discourse. (For instance, the national hate crimes bill passed recently did not include compiling incidents of male violence against women because "there would be too many of them.") Obvious because fear of men's violence laces our every decision. This fear does not have to be conscious to be effective. Most of us live in denial, and many women say they don't feel afraid, shaking their heads at the women who do. But ask if they walk alone at night or go to certain parts of the city unaccompanied or leave their windows open as they fall asleep, and you'll notice that the majority of women are aware, deep inside, that danger lurks just beyond the thin veil of their denial. The gender of that danger, you can be sure, is male.

In a recent survey of 4,450 respondents conducted by *Ms.* magazine,[2] three out of four women had experienced male violence; 83 percent knew at least one woman who had been raped, and only 7 percent of the respondents could say they had never experienced male violence and also say they did not know a rape victim. The implications of such numbers are staggering, and yet we do not stagger. We go on living our lives, enduring our own violent encounters with men as if we are the only women in the world who do. We are encouraged to write off male violence as the work of a few sick individuals. We are numbed by the numbers, and that is precisely the intention, to isolate and immobilize women. What else can we learn from these statistics?

The rules of grammar, one might think, are straightforward enough and unlikely to be twisted for political purposes, but propaganda is crafty, its purpose to manipulate and persuade through subtle, preferably undetectable means. In the case of statistics, consider what linguist Julia Penelope calls agent deletion: Take a common statistic, say, "Every four minutes, a woman is raped." What do you see? A woman, walking down the street perhaps, and suddenly—what? She *becomes* raped? Do you see the man jumping out from the shadow in that statement? No. You do not. With a grammatical sleight of hand, the agent is deleted, the man disappears, and you see only women, many of them, frequently and inexplicably raped. But change your focus and look again.

> Every four minutes, a man rapes a woman.
> Every fifteen seconds, a man beats a woman.

Suddenly men are in the picture. Lots of men. Men with something on their minds. Countless men raping, beating, and murdering women. (Refraining from such extremes, myriad others are leering at women, feeling up women on public transportation, telling sexist jokes, and otherwise sexually harassing women on the job or verbally demeaning them at home.) And *countless* would be the operative term here since my efforts to find statistics describing the numbers of men who commit violence against women, rather than the numbers of women who are victims of it, have been unsuccessful. If they were to be computed, these facts might sound something like, "One out of five men have raped at least one woman," or "Men commit twenty-one thousand acts of violence against women every week"—and thus a different picture would begin to emerge in public view. A fellow who works with male batterers suggested to me that the statistics are worded to focus on the victims instead of the perpetrators because this image, of so many violent and abusive men, is unbearable. (More so, I suppose, than so many dead and injured women.) The grammar of the statistics serves to distract us from the very image that might trigger our constructive and concerted outrage. With the agent deleted, we simply see women beaten, raped, and murdered. It just happens. A fact of life. The invisible obvious.

To look at the picture from another angle, we might turn to the natural world, to nonhuman creatures who rely on their instincts for survival. Some animals are natural enemies, such as owls and field mice, cats and birds, lions and gazelles. There are, we see, predators and prey. These are facts of life, and we can presume that such babies are taught early on which are predators and which are prey. Predators are avoided or fought: there is no in-between stance, no moral judgment, no plea for justice. Fight or flight. We can assume it is never suggested to gazelles that they cozy up to a lion or that field mice try reasoning with owls. You don't lobby for your rights with a natural enemy.

Of course, we are not talking about the so-called natural world, we are talking about civilized human beings, men and women. We are of the same species (or so we are taught), and thus it is painful to consider that one gender might be the natural enemy—the predator—of the other, although we can observe this phenomenon in a few other species. Could male violence against women be innate? Can it be that they cannot help themselves? If so, how would this knowledge change our attitude toward them? Would a biological predisposition somehow absolve them of responsibility (as if they take responsibility anyway)? However interesting it might be to speculate on reasons for this behavior, ultimately it is a moot point. The evidence is in. Men *act* like predators of women.

What activities would you do alone, at night?

go out for a walk

go jogging/running

drink at a bar

walk to a friend's house

see a movie

go grocery shopping

explore an unfamiliar neighborhood

speak with a stranger

I slip into my own denial like a familiar cardigan, pulling it close against fleeting chilly moments of awareness. I find such a moment in a journal entry, a decade old.

"July 1980. What to do about Rape Season? The summer heat, worst in thirty years, exacerbates my fear of attack. I sweat through the nights, recalling at random the recent stories of intruders who appear at the foot of the bed, having stolen in through an open window. My windows barred and shut, I finally admit that as the heat has little to do with the rape frequency, the bars on the window have little effect on my fear. One more story does it: She was walking to the grocery store three blocks from her house in my neighborhood. It was just dark, she saw a tall jogger approaching, and she stepped to the side of the walk to let him pass. As he came closer, she nodded and he nodded, and when he came even with her he stretched out his arm, took her by the neck, and as she screamed, he slit her throat. She dropped to the ground, found some long minutes later in a growing pool of blood. Everyone in the emergency room, the story goes, said he meant to kill her. She is not dead, but the new stitches reach from the hollow of her throat to her ear.

"All my rationalizations cannot explain away this knowledge: the violence is random, it is intentional, it is deadly, it is male. A new connection, a new frame of reference: questioning why the danger exists is a separate activity from protecting myself from the danger. Understanding why men taunt/rape/beat/kill women at random will not protect me from it. I know, finally, that I am never safe. I take action. I sign up for a workshop in self-defense.

"I will remember Marianna's voice, her presence, her strength, her warnings, her insistence in telling us we are strong, have the right to be strong, have the right to defend ourselves. Twenty-five women in a circle, telling each other why we are taking this course: I was beaten. I was attacked. I was abused as a child. I am being followed. I was raped. I am afraid to walk alone. I am tired of being afraid.

"Marianna teaches us to punch with our fists. I realize as I mold my hand to match hers and jab it into the padded bolster that I have never thrown a full blow. An entirely new sensation, the arm straight and true as an arrow, the fist landing squarely on target, the pad shuddering from the power of the impact. 'If you still think you are weak,' Marianna suggests, 'imagine what that much force would do to a face.' I fold my arms across my stomach and wince. It would hurt someone's face.

"Applying our new skills, we act out the familiar scenes: the parking deck, the bus stop, the walk from store to home. We create our nightmares, becoming the one with the gun, the one with the knife, we become the attacker, grabbing each other by the neck from behind. We learn to spin away, to yell from the gut, to punch, jab, kick, and throw. We learn to say, 'GET AWAY FROM ME. YOU HAVE NO RIGHT HERE.'

"I am stronger now because I know I can hurt someone who tries to hurt me. My body is not a handicap, some soft burden wrapped around a fierce core. I can defend my center if necessary. I know this now. By this awareness, this action, I transform my anger into protection. I cannot change the world of violence, but I can choose to change myself, and that act impacts my world."

Reading this entry ten years later, I am impressed with my clarity and commitment. Then I notice I have not pursued self-defense skills beyond that single weekend, preferring the comforts of denial to the disturbance of consciousness. I just want to live my life, do my work, and ignore the violence, the fear, and the anger.

Have you ever not done the following because you were afraid of violent consequences? (frequently, occasionally, never)

disagreed with spouse/lover

talked back to father

argued with an adult child

argued with boss

gotten drunk on a date

Of course, denial is at best a temporary solution. The violence continues, my anger increases, and like many women after seeing the film *Thelma and Louise*, I found myself harboring a secret longing for a gun. I envied their bold responses to men's disgusting behavior that left some guys cowering and another one dead. My philosophical and spiritual commitment to nonviolence was challenged by my joyful burst of shameless gratitude when Louise deftly put the insidious rapist away. Justice! How refreshing. Their bravado enlivened the outrage I keep bridled somewhere between my heart and my gut, and for the first time I wondered quite frankly why most women, myself included, don't carry guns. So I began to ask.

Over six months, I talked to women all over the country and solicited their opinions on women and guns. Their responses ranged from complete rejection of guns to a cool and practiced use of them. I found my own reactions telling: just as something about Thelma's chirpy armed robbery and Louise's resigned murder of the rapist thrilled me, "real-life" women who feel at ease with both the need for and the use of guns elicited from me a kind of shock. Women are not supposed to do this kind of thing, I hear in my mind.

Do you now carry (circle all that apply):

gun   knife   pocketknife or something sharp   mace   whistle

The young woman from Texas is matter-of-fact when I ask if she uses a gun. Certainly, she says. She learned to use a shotgun as a girl and keeps one in her rural home. Her work requires frequent road trips across desolate Texas plains, so she has a pistol for the car. And lately, she adds, she's been wanting to do some long-distance bicycling. "I might get a little Beretta," she says as if talking about a certain pair of shoes. "I wouldn't consider biking alone without a gun," she adds. I am staring, dumbstruck by her casual acceptance of weaponry. I ask how she came to feel this way. She looks at me straight on, her eyes narrow slightly, and she shrugs. "It's a war out there. Men against women. I'm not about to go around undefended. That would be stupid."

Many women who carry guns began doing so after experiences of being personally attacked, and many women who are against the use of guns suspect their feelings might change if they were attacked. The results of my random survey revealed a variety of reasons why women don't carry guns: they don't know how to use one and don't want to/don't feel they can learn; they fear a gun will be used against them by an assailant; they don't want to use "male" methods; they don't believe in the use of violence. This divergence among women seems to be related to shedding the veil of denial. Considering the prevalence of male violence against women, to remain unprepared does seem—in the words of the young Texas woman—stupid.

Stories from women who are prepared—by training in the use of guns, for instance—amazed me. Some of them were in law enforcement. Because the nature of their job removes the taboo from women using weapons, essentially "allowing" women to become proficient with guns, the power differential I am accustomed to between men and women is turned on its head. A national park ranger related this story:

"My first week on the job I did a felony car stop on a man who was running from the local police. I ordered him to get out of the car. He waited and then made a quick movement to his waistband. I had been aiming the shotgun in his general direction, and when he moved I put a shell in the chamber and waited to see if he pulled out a gun. The sound of the shotgun's action convinced him to get out of the car with his hands up and his pants wet! He told me later he was so scared that he couldn't keep from wetting his pants."

In another instance, a woman was pulled over on a rural road by a car with flashing lights, which she assumed was a policeman. When the uniformed man pushed her down on the front seat and began to rape her, she managed to pull out her gun from underneath the seat and shoot him. She then pushed him out on the highway, drove to the emergency room of the nearest hospital, and turned herself in. He was not, as it turned out, a policeman, but a serial rapist. She was his eighth known victim.

I must admit that the image in the first story of a man being that scared of a woman appeals to me, and the evidence in both stories that a woman can learn to use a gun is reassuring. Like many women, I imagine myself being hopelessly inept with such a device, despite the fact that I have demonstrated a high level of manual dexterity with other more complex tools. My assumption, that I could not learn to use a gun, was echoed with such frequency throughout my interviews with women that I suspect it is based not on experience or personal knowledge but stems instead from the propaganda that tells us what is appropriate behavior for women. Naming the prevalence of male violence is not tactful, self-defense is not ladylike, and retaliation is utterly monstrous.

The truck driver who repeatedly taunts Thelma and Louise with obscene gestures from the cab of his gleaming semi goes slightly mad when instead of shooting him they elect to blow up his precious truck. As the vehicle explodes in flames and the women drive off, he shakes his fist and calls them bitches from hell. This, I think, is the category men reserve for women who in any way acknowledge or resist male violence.

I could justify killing (1. yes, 2. no, 3. don't know)

someone trying to rape me

convicted serial killer

someone attempting murder

Adolf Hitler

Yet Audre Lorde has reminded us that we cannot dismantle the master's house using the master's tools. Many women responded to my query with similar feelings, saying they do not want to condone the use of violence. "To match an enemy, we become no better than he. You can only gain peace by being peaceful," said one woman. "I want 'claiming my power' to mean something very different from the male model," said another. In a group discussion during a women's music festival, a woman described her belief that resorting to violence obscures the connection to our unique female powers and is against our basic peaceful nature. By remaining true to ourselves, she suggested, our womanly ways will eventually overwhelm the culture of male violence we now endure, creating a society of peace, safety, and mutual respect.

All these principles are true enough, and certainly more noble than my occasional sordid fantasies of using cattle prods to herd violent men into re-education camps. As a feminist, I agree that the means are the ends. I am disturbed by the prospect of women taking up arms. I, too, dream of a world without violence. However, I cannot fail to notice that at the moment, we're apparently in a rather long and awkward transition period between patriarchal hell and that feminist utopia. The particular era to which we are consigned requires that we contend with the reality of male violence against women. In the face of this clear and present danger, I wonder once again, what's a principled gal to do?

What precautions do you take to stay safe?

walk in pairs whenever possible
have house keys at the ready
check car before getting in
always watch who is around
take self-defense classes
carry purse strapped to body so it won't be stolen
avoid wearing clothing that could restrict movement
never put telephone number on checks

The issue of self-defense caused even the women most fervently against the use of guns to waiver. Nearly every woman described encounters with violent men when she wished she'd had a gun, or said she was sure if she'd had one, she would have used it. Yet a minority of women I talked to have self-defense training of any sort. I ponder again why the obvious need for self-defense does not motivate more women to carry a weapon, practice a martial art, or otherwise learn to protect ourselves. In this strange jigsaw puzzle, there seems to be a missing piece.

The invisible obvious dawns on me slowly. One of the main symptoms of sustained oppression, I have learned from feminist theory, is the destruction of a sense of self. Characteristically, oppressed people exhibit low self-esteem, low self-worth, a lack of identity. As we absorb the oppressor's relentless messages about our inferiority, we come to believe them. Could it be that as women in a woman-hating society, we do not feel we have a self to defend? Such a belief would make "women's self-defense" an oxymoron. In a peculiar twist, agent deletion strikes again.

Self-defense is a pragmatic and necessary extension of self-love, self-respect, and self-determination. Self-defense does not contradict a commitment to nonviolence. While the form of self-defense is up to the individual woman, the need for self-defense is unquestionable. Carry Mace, learn akido, always wear shoes you can run in, stay alert—whatever you choose to do to protect yourself within the context of your own principled integrity, do it. Beyond the obvious need for self-protection, there is another, perhaps even more important, reason to take action.

Women deserve to live in safety and dignity. Male violence against women in any form is unacceptable. Our righteous outrage on behalf of our own precious selves must lead us first to take measures to insure our personal survival. To build a utopia, it helps to be alive.

Afterword

Deborah Brink, after reading this essay, created the Oath of the Bitches from Hell:

I pledge to raise Holy Hell
For the sake of my Self and my Sisters.
I will continue to take back my power,
And take back the night,
And no man will ever feel safe
To harm any woman again.

NOTES

1   All survey questions taken from *Ms.* 1, 2 (1990).

2   For the survey itself, see *Ms.* 1, 2 (1990). For survey results, see *Ms.* 1, 5 (1991).

Responses

Personally I like guns. Yeah. Embarrassing sentiment, I know. In the late 1960s early 1970s when the new wave womyns movement emerged, drawing many of us from the civil rights and antiwar movements/training grounds, we were already instilled with "nonviolent" values. And we applied them, pasted them onto our feminist movement. So I think we do need to question this value. Each one of us. Consider our situation and needs and beliefs. I sold my revolver when my mom died and I needed money to live. Haven't replaced it, though I miss going to the firing range. All in all, I prefer dogs as a defense. It has worked well for me, so far. Still, the sheer power of a gun is alluring. Dangerous. When a group of womyn took a gun safety class together one summer when a rapist attacked dozens of us, unhindered by police or anyone else, we were scared. Scared because eight or nine politically active womyn were learning to fire guns. Scared because we enjoyed it. We'd go eat pizza together after each session to talk about our reactions. The conflicts inherent in our meetings to plan nonviolent demonstrations on Tuesday and our Wednesday gun class—that was a rush. We each must decide, must remember, there is a war on. I wish there were a simple answer.

Leslita, Archer, FL

I had dinner with a friend at a restaurant. At one point, she said she was hot. I suggested she take off her sweatshirt. She started to, stopped; her cheeks blushed. I asked if she wasn't wearing anything underneath. She shook her head, her left hand reached to her side and carefully raised her sweatshirt. I looked down to see a handgun. I smiled. We went on with our evening.

Why did she have the gun? Her life is threatened, and unlike many women who will not consider owning a weapon until they are a "victim," my friend has chosen to take whatever steps she can to prevent the assault.

My reaction? I am quite aware of the specific level of danger in my friend's life. It is her status quo, and she functions on the defensive. As her friend, I support her choice to protect herself and to stay alive. Were I in her situation I would probably do the same.

What was provoking about your essay is the predisposition of women to remove themselves from the identity of one who is threatened. It is obvious that as women we are threatened. What separates me from my friend is the specific articulation of the danger. It is articulated to the point that it can no longer be ignored. Victims can no longer ignore the danger because they carry wounds, emotional and physical, current and in memory (as well as those promised).

The natural world is one of survival. In our "civilized" society we artificially remove ourselves (intellectually and emotionally) from the dangers that are a part of our daily lives. . . . Some people prefer to consider themselves other than animal—above animals. It is an arrogant elitism.

Maytee Aspuro, Madison, WI

A group of us is moving, at long last, toward rural lesbian community. For the past several years while dreaming this, I've pondered the feelings I've had for the necessity of protection. I've always considered myself an extreme pacifist, except for those midnight fantasies of retaliating for rape and the three times I leapt from my seat applauding the scenes in *Thelma and Louise* that you referred to. I'm not real happy with these responses.

I've allowed myself limitless abundance in my dreams for community. Doing physical violence, even to protect myself and loved ones, just doesn't fit. I don't want it to. So much of the reason for creating our own social security is to live in what we believe can be true, even if we don't see it in the rest of the world. I choose to believe that we can live in love.

So last month I reread *Journey to Zelindar* by Diana River, and there appeared what I would like to believe is the answer: that womyn have the (psychic) power to deflect the violence that men direct toward us. This power may be latent, to varying degrees, in all of us. But I know it's there. It may not be possible to see it fully developed in my lifetime, but I figure it's worth a try. At some level, in some cell, we already know how.

Barb Parks, Huntsville, AL

Self-defense is so very reasonable. I think self-determination and self-defense go hand in hand. Sometimes I do wonder whether we, as women, are suffering even now from some sort of collective shock from the witch burnings? Granted, not all our antecedents are European, but other cultures seemed to have spawned woman-hating, too.

I don't believe that violence is the key to self-defense, although confrontations can occur in which you do need to employ physical force. I believe that self-defense starts with self-esteem and is in keeping with personal integrity.

I have noticed, however, an aversion to self-defense because it has the possibility of involving violence. Is this aversion at all tied to our massive collective suffering that Western civilization to this day fails to acknowledge?

Name withheld by request

Women are valued for "womanly" qualities of compassion, gentleness, and yes, of course, nonviolence. One of my political phases that I thought would never end, the part that was so obviously really me and not conditioning (I thought), was pacifism.

Studying violence against women brought me up against this "true self" again and again. Asking "Who benefits?" (from my pacifism) again and again, it was clear that the oppressor benefits. It's certainly easier to terrorize women if even the most alert, discriminating, and critical ones in the bunch can't imagine perpetrating physical violence against their oppressors without their souls splitting in two.

On and on it goes. Would I initiate violence against a man? Probably not, any more than I would initiate conversation. Would I kill a man trying to rape me? Not my first choice, but if that's what it took, of course. Do I have the skills to fight back? No. So thanks for the review of the reasons to learn. My feminism is my way of being fearless in the worlds of work, talk, ideas, etc. Time to forge the tools I need on the street. Anything less starts to sound like denial.

. . . We are not necessarily co-opting a boy-toy when we explore our ability to fight, fight back, use weapons. We are, though, violating the boundaries men have put on our imaginations. During the burning times, some women had to give in, had to agree to the rules, odious and mind-numbing as they were, or there just wouldn't have been any women left. Consciously or not, some had to do this.

This time around, our burning times, we have different options, and some of us must explore approaches to survival that many of us find odious. When I finally started thinking about violence, killing, physical harm in a new way, it wasn't a revenge thing. It was more like, "You guys took something out of my brain and heart and I'm gonna put it back. I may not hurt you, but I'm gonna put it back. I'm gonna take away your guarantee."

Judith Angelo, Cleveland Heights, OH

Re-asking your question, "Do I believe I have a self to defend?" the answer blazingly propelled me to sign up for a self-defense class.

In reading *The Chalice and the Blade*, I was struck by the magnitude and deep-rooted basis of society's beliefs that womyn do not have the right to take revenge or to exert power. As Joan Rockwell, author of *Fact in Fiction*, writes, "If a mighty creature like Clytemnestra (in the Greek drama *Oresteia*) with the provocation she has in the murder of her child Iphigenia has not the right to take revenge, what woman has?" The intent of *Oresteia* was to promote patrilineal descent and to silence womyn from even thinking of doing rebellious acts. I then realized that it is/was no surprise that many people in our patriarchal society were up in arms over *Thelma and Louise*. They believe that they, not womyn, have the right to bear arms. Thanks for challenging my beliefs and changing my behavior to defend my self.

Kit Hoffmann, Yarmouth, MA

A random thought someone passed on to me during this past year of pondering these issues: If it is true that violence begets violence, then it follows that women would be very violent people. My question: Does the largely nonviolent response of women to male violence show that we are innately peaceful beings, or that our collective will has been broken?

Kay

The Habit of Freedom:
Liberating the Colonized Mind

A counselor specializing in midlife transitions for women startled me a few years ago when she confided that she had stopped telling her clients to love themselves. "That was absolutely the wrong advice," she told me. When I recovered from my surprise enough to ask what she was suggesting to women instead, she said, "I tell them to *act* like they love themselves. I realized that in this culture, if a woman waits until she actually loves herself to act that way, it may never happen."

Indeed. For me, her paradoxical advice sums up both the problem and solution imposed by the conundrum of oppression: Because we are taught to hate ourselves, and since self-hatred insures both our collusion with the system of dominance and its continued success, then in order to stop the cycle in our own lives and to transform society as a whole, we must begin to love ourselves—or at least act as if we do. Speaking in these abstractions, however, the process seems as simpleminded as a bumper sticker: Act Like You Love Yourself—Until You Do. Or, I ♥ Myself . . . Really! followed, of course, by a smiley face. I am reminded of comedian Linda Moakes's definition: Affirmations are lies I tell myself until I believe them. If the solution were so simple, however, I wouldn't be writing this essay, and we'd all be busy experiencing creative fulfillment in the feminist utopia.

Virginia Woolf outlined the dilemma a different way in her classic treatise on women and creativity, *A Room of One's Own*. After describing in great detail the history of social and political obstacles faced by women, Woolf concludes that even if a woman has "five hundred pounds a year and a room of her own"—that is, adequate money, time, and privacy—her creativity will remain undeveloped unless she also practices "the habit of freedom." Since women have lived restricted lives for so long, she observes, we are not accustomed to freedom, and even when we establish an encouraging environment, freedom is not automatic or comfortable for most of us. Instead it is something we must consciously choose and then practice. At the time she wrote this, in 1929, Woolf thought perhaps a century of optimum conditions and serious commitment might show some results. With thirty-odd years to go, I feel a need to pick up the pace. Although women have made great strides over the past six decades (after all, many of us are now allowed to vote, read, own property, and in some instances receive payment for our labor), I believe our collective creative genius remains virtually untapped. It's time to move on to the next phase. I want to practice the habit of freedom.

It's hard to fight an enemy who has outposts in your head.

Sally Kempton[1]

To understand the habit of freedom—what it is, exactly, and how to do it—a deeper appreciation for our present condition might be helpful. How *are* women convinced to collude in our own oppression? Some analysts have compared the socialization of women to the domestication of animals, and I have found the analogy to be at once profoundly useful and enormously disturbing.[2] Proceed with caution. Freedom is not for the faint of heart.

Imagine a homesteader somewhere on the great plains in the last century who determines a need for horses. He decides to capture some feral creatures from the high mountain desert and turn them into draft animals, trained to do work for humans. These first recruits are understandably reluctant, and the farmer has great difficulty hitching the horses to the plow, much less getting them to pull it. The animals have no inclination to do human work; indeed they constantly attempt to flee, and they resist the harnesses, bridles, and bits. Eventually, after much effort, the farmer is able to break their will sufficiently, and the fields are finally plowed. These are not, however, the best draft animals the farmer will ever have.

When the first foal is born, the farmer begins. As soon as the tiny horse stands up, the farmer places some strips of leather over her back, not cinching or tying them in any way, but simply creating the sensation of weight, however slight. Soon he belts them lightly beneath the belly, and after the foal becomes used to this, he slides a bridle—but no bit—over her head, letting the reins lay loosely on her neck. As the weeks go by, gradually and with great care the farmer introduces the various tools and bindings that will allow him to harness the horse's energy and direct it to his will, his work. This is an education of sorts, the farmer creating a world for this horse that is vastly different from the world of her parents, who have a memory of freedom. Under this training, the horse becomes an excellent draft animal, docile, tolerant, and yielding, with no thoughts other than those he has placed in her mind. The farmer is very pleased, and he names her Bessie. This process is repeated for many generations, until the farmer is renowned for his superb draft animals, and his stable is filled with obedience.

It should be noted that as animals are trained in this way, their musculature and skeletal structure actually begin to conform to the harnesses, bridles, and other restrictions, so that over time the trainer succeeds in altering their physical, as well as their mental, being. Although the transformation by this taming process is gradual, it is ultimately quite thorough.[3]

Taking a moment to reflect on this analogy, we can see how the socialization of women to accept and collude with male domination has also been a gradual and thorough process. We are not born into this world innocent and wild with minds full of freedom but as heirs to some five thousand years of "education." Surely, our bodies must remember the effects of the corsets, girdles, stays, hoop skirts, painful shoes, and other restrictions that harnessed centuries of our foresisters to the whims of men.[4] Today we continue to starve or stuff ourselves, pare away or pump up parts of ourselves, in order to conform, or to grieve for failing to conform to those same whims. Our minds are colonized by values that destroy our creativity, freedom, and will. Our hearts bear the scars of ancient rape. In other words, the compliant nature of women is a creation many generations in the making, and our memory of freedom is a product of imagination, not experience. A further subtlety to ponder is the rather obvious fact that if male dominance were natural, there would be no need for the extensive systems of coercion to enforce it.

Back on our hypothetical farm, years go by. The farmer dies, leaving his property to his only child, a daughter. She is a radical feminist, having left the farm early on to pursue her interests at a university in Wisconsin, Michigan, or California, and she's been to her share of womyn's festivals. When she returns to take care of the family business, she looks out at the stable of obedience and thinks, "This is my farm now. These horses are captives! This is dominance and subordination, and I'll not have it." With revolutionary zeal, she marches down to the corral and sees Bessie, old and tired now, as tame as a horse could ever be. The daughter remembers the horse from her childhood and aches for the years of servitude Bessie has endured. She opens the corral gate wide. "You can go, now, girl. You can be free!"

The daughter waits expectantly for the horse to trot through the gate, back to the high mountain desert of freedom. But Bessie does not move. She does not trot through the gate. She waits for instruction, she wants to know when the next work shift begins, and when the next meal will be put out. She does not move toward the freedom beyond the corral. She does not know what lies outside the gate.

Frustrated and bewildered, the daughter realizes that in order to free the horses, she can't just let them go. She must teach them what freedom is. In fact if she takes them out to the wilderness and leaves them, they will die, for their knowledge of how

to take care of themselves has been erased. They are domesti-
cated, tamed, dependent. Like her father, the daughter must re-
educate the horses, but her task is to gradually introduce them
to freedom and the skills that will enable them to survive. Bessie
will probably never leave the corral for good, but she can enjoy a
life without harnesses and spend long afternoons wandering
around the prairie. The daughter will start with the young ones,
taking them to the high mountain desert to roam for days at a
time, leaving oats and hay near the stream. Gradually the horses
will learn about freedom, and the next generations will be different.

For women, the corral is the patriarchal construction of
gender. It has surrounded us for over five thousand years. We
cannot fathom what lies beyond a society consigning women to
inferiority through its laws, institutions, and customs. For most
of us, the prospect of leaving this corral is terrifying, and right-
fully so: It is all we know. Without our harnesses, our bridles,
bits, and saddles, we do not know what to do or who we are.
Faced with the open-ended mystery of freedom, often the mis-
ery we know is preferable if only for the comfort of its familiar-
ity. There are stories of circus elephants, accustomed to being
tied to a post, who never venture beyond the circumference of
the rope even when it is removed. After hearing the draft animal
analogy, a workshop participant said with great pain that her
dog would carry its leash to her when it wanted to go out, never
thinking it could go outside unleashed.

Admittedly the draft animal analogy is grim, intended to at-
tune us to the fact that women did not arrive at this point
overnight or even over a few generations. This knowledge gives
our struggle the dimension and dignity of history, and in view of

it we do not expect to overturn our situation quickly. This awareness helps cultivate a certain compassionate patience alongside our urgency when working for change, both in society and in ourselves.

But women are not draft animals, and comparing our socialization to the domestication of horses does break down at a crucial, heartening point. Speaking of women, Marilyn Frye notes, "Unlike nonhuman animals, this one matches the exploiter in intelligence and fineness of physical abilities, and this one is capable of self-respect, righteousness and resentment."[5] I take this to mean that despite our legacy of oppression, our context of domination, and our colonized minds, women are capable at any moment of choosing to practice the habit of freedom.

> *We all need to make a conscious break with the system.*
>
> bell hooks[6]

I have been the farmer's radical daughter, and I have felt her impatience toward myself and other women. In the late 1970s, after consuming large quantities of radical feminist thought (Mary Daly, Adrienne Rich, Susan Griffin, Audre Lorde, Andrea Dworkin, and others), I felt a surge of ironic liberty having finally grasped the existence of institutionalized sexism. An epiphanal frenzy followed this insight, and I declared I was no longer a fembot, a slave to the culture, a colonized mind, but a free woman. I had seen the corral's gate, and I was outta there. It was history. Period. End of patriarchy. Simple. Or so I thought.

I was disappointed to discover that despite my astute intellectual grasp of the situation, in the privacy of my thoughts, feelings, and dreams, the oppressor still influenced me. I continued to act like a good workhorse when left to my automatic responses, my habits. They kept me steeped in self-hatred and obedient to the core. Clearly there was more work to be done. Recognizing the unjust system was just the beginning. Much like the farmer who constructed a new reality for the horses he wanted to tame, and the daughter who wanted to free them, I needed to create a support system for the new way of being I had claimed. To the extent that I was able to perceive it, collusion was no longer an acceptable option.

Suddenly I became as fascinated with my daily routines as a traveler in a foreign country. I began an intimate scavenger hunt, looking for clues that would crack the code of my conditioning. Where was my harness, my bridle, my bit? Who were the uninvited guests lodged in my mind, and what were they telling me? What messages was I incorporating—literally—without scrutinizing their meaning? How did I carry my leash to the door? In the subtle web of my daily choices, I discovered profound opportunities for practicing the habit of freedom. Each small, conscious shift from automatic obedience to self-determination thrilled me. Mary Daly has named this process Roboticide.[7]

One of the first areas to come under my scrutiny was clothing. I decided I would wear only clothes that were absolutely comfortable—no cinching waistbands, no high-heeled shoes, no awkward but fashionable styles. I would not don my own harness, bridle, or bit. On a physical level, I refused to give my body the message of restriction or discomfort merely to win acceptance. I was amazed at two things: how deeply satisfying this daily act of rebellion was, and how little difference it made to the people around me. That is, choices I made to conform to some imagined standard were largely unnecessary.

Another daily experience that came under my scrutiny was conversations with men. I noticed how often men interrupted me, and how I was programmed to defer without comment.[8] My psychic bit removed, I encouraged myself to interrupt their interruptions, to say, simply, "I'd like to finish my comment." Once again I was amazed that the world did not come crashing down as I exercised my freedom to speak and my right to be heard. Instead, more often than not, men apologized and listened.

I found simple acts of self-nurture to have startling power. For a while I bought a single cut flower each week and placed it on the dinner table or nightstand so I could watch it blossom and smell its fragrance. At first I could hardly tolerate such reckless indulgence, but the minor expense purchased a powerful message: I deserve beauty. Making time for long baths, preparing healthful meals, and conscientiously muting the commercials on television or choosing not to watch it at all contributed to a personal environment of encouragement and clarity.[9]

My journal took on special significance during this time. Recording my experiments with the habit of freedom, I began to notice the script of my internalized oppressor. It was the relentless inner critic saying, "Who the hell do you think you are? You'll never succeed. Don't dare talk back. Get back in line!" These admonitions echoed messages absorbed from the misogynist culture, and I realized that the internal critic—to whom I felt so responsible—was in fact on the payroll of the patriarchy. Each time I sent the inner critic to the time-out chair, I was able to evoke the loving aspects of my essential self—the intelligent skeptic, the wise elder, and the angel of optimism.[10] Before long, the patriarchal values I had unwittingly internalized no longer had a bullhorn inside my head.

The habit of freedom, then, is the essential self in action. As the draft horse sheds her harness, we shed our obedience to the culture of domination and follow the voice of our own integrity out the gate. Each one of us must necessarily do this for ourselves, but we needn't go it alone. Beyond the confines of the corral, we must find one another to create a community of affirmation, encouragement, celebration, and pleasure, where we can be lovingly challenged to develop our full potential. As Gloria Steinem suggests, "If women have just begun to realize how deeply our self-esteem has been undermined by centuries of woman-hating cultures, perhaps only the constant presence in our lives of a woman-loving group can help us believe in our authentic selves."[11]

> *The point is . . . to imagine women not enslaved, to*
> *imagine these intelligent, willful and female bodies*
> *not subordinated in service to males, individually or*
> *via institutions (or to anybody, in any way); not*
> *pressed into a shape that suits an arrogant eye.*
>
> Marilyn Frye[12]

How would an untamed human female act? What would she look like? How would she make decisions, and on what basis? The image of such a creature is almost impossible to imagine, yet if we are to become free women, we must learn to imagine the impossible. With a defiant leap of faith, we break the closed circuit of collusion and oppression when we begin to love ourselves—or at least act as if we do.

The transformation from fembot to hothead may start with an epiphany, but liberating the colonized mind is in fact a lifelong endeavor. The habit of freedom, much like the automatic obedience it replaces, is the outward manifestation of an internalized value system; but this one must be chosen consciously, meticulously, moment by moment. It is the global paradigm shift of values we long for, up close and personal. At first these increments of mindful change may seem infinitesimal, but practicing the habit of freedom has a cumulative effect. Its ultimate expression is revolution.

Not long ago, I awoke from a dream, a perplexing image that lingered in my mind until I followed it. What I saw was a group of women, running. I think of course they must be running from some danger, but as I watch them more carefully, I see they are not afraid. Their faces are full of joy, and they are running together solely for the pleasure of feeling the wind on their bodies. Where they are, there is nothing to fear.

NOTES

1 Sally Kempton, "Cutting Loose," reprinted in *About Women,* ed. Stephen Berg and S. J. Marks (New York: Fawcett, 1973).

2 See Marilyn Frye, "In and out of Harm's Way: On Arrogance and Love," in *The Politics of Reality: Essays in Feminist Theory;* and Susan Griffin, *Woman and Nature.* Readers familiar with these works will recognize the roots of their brilliant analyses in this essay. To those who work lovingly with animals, know that I appreciate your intentions (especially with dogs!) and do not mean to disparage them.

3 I am grateful to Annie Conn for information about horse training.

4 My own distant cousin Cornelia Willson died at age twenty-four in 1860 from asphyxiation when she tied the lacings of her corset too tightly, pulling them from a bedpost. "Stovepipe" waists were much admired at the time (Evie Sartor Byrd, "Highlights of Family History 1700–1952," private paper).

5   Frye, "In and Out of Harm's Way," 59.

6   bell hooks, "Feminist Revolution: Development Through Struggle," in *Feminist Theory: From Margin to Center* (Boston: South End Press, 1984).

7   Mary Daly, *Gyn/Ecology: The Metaethics of Radical Feminism* (Boston: Beacon Press, 1978, 1990), 56.

8   For a thorough guide to conversational politics, see Deborah Tannen, *You Just Don't Understand* (New York: Ballantine, 1990).

9   See Jennifer Louden, *The Women's Comfort Book* (San Francisco: HarperSanFrancisco, 1992), for a compendium of self-nurturing suggestions.

10 See my first book, *Internal Affairs: A Journalkeeping Guidebook for Self-Intimacy*, for more information (San Francisco: HarperSanFrancisco, 1990).

11 Gloria Steinem, "Helping Ourselves to Revolution," *Ms.* 3, 3:29, and *Revolution from Within: The Politics of Self-Esteem* (New York: Little, Brown, 1992).

12 Frye, "In and Out of Harm's Way," 76.

Afterword

Because the subscribers to the *Fugitive Information* essay series had yet to receive "The Habit of Freedom" at the time this manuscript was completed, their responses could not be included here. However, the interactive spirit of this project suggests that this is as it should be, for it creates the opportunity for readers of this book to contribute to the evolution of the ideas presented here.

I invite readers' responses to any of the essays, especially "The Habit of Freedom," and although I cannot always answer letters, I eagerly read each one and depend on them to test and strengthen my work. I am gathering information about "heart sisters"—ongoing women's groups for consciousness-raising, personal growth, networking, emotional support, etc.—for a possible book and directory, and would appreciate hearing from women involved in such circles.

I also invite readers to join the web of subscribers to *Fugitive Information,* the continuing essay series and newsletter on which this book is based.

Please address correspondence and requests for information about subscriptions or my touring schedule to: Escapadia Press, P.O. Box 22262, Santa Fe, NM 87505-22262. For electronic mail, khag@well.sf.ca.us.

Related Resources

Volt Lives! Diary of a Hothead

Anderson, Bonnie S., and Judith P. Zinsser. *A History of Their Own: Women in Europe from Prehistory to the Present.* Vols. 1 & 2. New York: Harper & Row, 1989.

Avrich, Paul. *An American Anarchist: The Life of Voltairine de Cleyre.* Princeton, NJ: Princeton Univ. Press, 1978.

DiMassa, Diane. *Hothead Paisan: Homicidal Lesbian Terrorist.* Vols. 1–7. Giant Ass Publishing, P.O. Box 214, New Haven, CT 06502. A radically witty political 'zine, not for the faint of heart.

Drakulić, Slavenka. *How We Survived Communism and Even Laughed.* New York: W. W. Norton, 1991.

Echols, Alice. *Daring to Be Bad: Radical Feminism in America 1967–1975.* Minneapolis: Univ. of Minnesota Press, 1989.

Edgerly, Lois Stiles. *Give Her This Day: A Daybook of Women's Words*. Gardiner, ME: Tilbury House, 1990.

Falk, Candace. *Love, Anarchy, and Emma Goldman*. New Brunswick, NJ: Rutgers Univ. Press, 1990.

French, Marilyn. *The War Against Women*. New York: Summit Books, 1991.

Fritz, Leah. *Dreamers and Dealers: An Intimate Appraisal of the Women's Movement*. Boston: Beacon Press, 1979.

Marsh, Margaret S. *Anarchist Women 1870–1920*. Philadelphia: Temple Univ. Press, 1981.

Codependency and the Myth of Recovery

Beattie, Melody. *Codependent No More*. New York: HarperCollins, 1987.

Frye, Marilyn. *The Politics of Reality: Essays in Feminist Theory*. Freedom, CA: Crossing Press, 1983.

Kasl, Charlotte Davis. *Many Roads, One Journey: Moving Beyond the Twelve Steps*. New York: HarperCollins, 1992.

Rich, Adrienne. *Of Woman Born: Motherhood as Experience and Institution*. New York: Bantam, 1977.

Sanford, Linda Tschirhart, and Mary Ellen Donovan. *Women and Self-Esteem: Understanding and Improving the Way We Think and Feel*. New York: Viking Penguin, 1985.

Schaef, Anne Wilson. *When Society Becomes an Addict*. San Francisco: Harper & Row, 1987.

———. *Women's Reality: An Emerging Female System in the White Male Society*. Minneapolis: Winston Press, 1981.

Subby, Robert, and John Friel. *Codependency: An Emerging Issue*. Pompano Beach, FL: Health Communications, 1984.

Wegscheider-Cruse, Sharon. *Another Chance: Hope and Health for the Alcoholic Family*. Palo Alto, CA: Science & Behavior, 1981.

Women's Counseling Referral and Education Centre. *Helping Ourselves: A Handbook for Women Starting Groups.* Toronto, Ont.: Women's Press, 1985.

The Wilderness of Intimacy: Control and Connection

Davison, Robyn. *Tracks.* New York: Pantheon, 1983.

Griffin, Susan. *Woman and Nature: The Roaring Inside Her.* New York: Harper & Row, 1978.

Gruen, Arno. *The Betrayal of the Self: The Fear of Autonomy in Men and Women.* New York: Grove Press, 1986.

Keller, Catherine. *From a Broken Web: Separation, Sexism, and Self.* Boston: Beacon Press, 1986.

Mander, Jerry. *In the Absence of the Sacred: The Failure of Technology and the Survival of the Indian Nations.* San Francisco: Sierra Club, 1991.

Seed, John, Joanna Macy, Pat Fleming, and Arne Naess. *Thinking Like a Mountain: Towards a Council of All Beings.* Philadelphia: New Society, 1988.

Orchids in the Arctic: The Predicament of Heterosexual Feminism

Atkinson, Ti-Grace. *Amazon Odyssey.* New York: Links Books, 1974.

Dworkin, Andrea. *Intercourse.* New York: Macmillan, 1987.

Hagan, Kay Leigh, ed. *Women Respond to the Men's Movement: A Feminist Collection.* San Francisco: HarperSanFrancisco, 1992.

Hoagland, Sarah Lucia. *Lesbian Ethics: Toward New Value.* Palo Alto, CA: Institute of Lesbian Studies, 1988.

Rich, Adrienne. "Compulsory Heterosexuality and the Lesbian Existence." In *Blood, Bread, and Poetry: Selected Prose 1979–1985.* New York: W. W. Norton, 1986.

Stoltenberg, John. *Refusing to Be a Man.* Portland, OR: Breitenbush Books, 1989.

The Invisible Obvious

Atwood, Margaret. *The Handmaid's Tale.* New York: Fawcett, 1985.

Daly, Mary. *Pure Lust: Elemental Feminist Philosophy.* Boston: Beacon Press, 1984.

Dworkin, Andrea. *Right Wing Women.* New York: G. P. Putnam, 1983.

————. *Woman Hating.* New York: E. P. Dutton, 1974.

Eisler, Riane. *The Chalice and the Blade: Our History, Our Future.* San Francisco: Harper & Row, 1987.

Faludi, Susan. *Backlash: The Undeclared War on American Women.* New York: Crown, 1991.

Freire, Paolo. *Pedagogy of the Oppressed.* New York: Continuum, 1986.

French, Marilyn. *Beyond Power: On Women, Men, and Morals.* New York: Summit Books, 1985.

Frye, Marilyn. *The Politics of Reality: Essays in Feminist Theory.* Freedom, CA: Crossing Press, 1983.

Gimbutas, Marija. *Goddesses and Gods of Old Europe.* San Francisco: HarperSanFrancisco, 1991.

Goleman, Daniel. *Vital Lies, Simple Truths: The Psychology of Self-Deception.* New York: Simon & Schuster, 1985.

Gray, Elizabeth Dodson. *Patriarchy as a Conceptual Trap.* Wellesley, MA: Roundtable Press, 1982.

Janeway, Elizabeth. *Powers of the Weak.* New York: Alfred A. Knopf, 1980.

Lerner, Gerda. *The Creation of Patriarchy.* New York: Oxford Univ. Press, 1986.

Nelson, Joyce. *The Perfect Machine: TV in the Nuclear Age.* Toronto: Between the Lines, 1987.

Pharr, Suzanne. *Homophobia: A Weapon of Sexism.* Inverness, CA: Chardon Press, 1988.

Pratkanis, Anthony, and Elliot Aronson. *Age of Propaganda: The Everyday Use and Abuse of Persuasion.* New York: W. H. Freeman & Co., 1991.

Sjöö, Monica, and Barbara Mor. *The Great Cosmic Mother.* San Francisco: HarperSanFrancisco, 1991.

Starhawk. *Dreaming the Dark: Magic, Sex, and Politics.* Boston: Beacon Press, 1982.

————. *Truth or Dare: Encounters with Power, Authority, and Mystery.* San Francisco: Harper & Row, 1987.

Tart, Charles. *Waking Up: Overcoming the Obstacles to Human Potential.* Boston: Shambhala, 1986.

Wittig, Monique. *The Straight Mind and Other Essays.* Boston: Beacon Press, 1992.

Heart Sisters: Loving Each Other over Time

Daly, Mary. *Gyn/Ecology: The Metaethics of Radical Feminism.* Boston: Beacon Press, 1978, 1990.

French, Marilyn. *Beyond Power: On Women, Men, and Morals.* New York: Summit Books, 1985.

Hart, Nett. *Spirited Lesbians: Lesbian Desire as Social Action.* Minneapolis: Word Weavers, 1989.

Hoagland, Sarah Lucia. *Lesbian Ethics: Toward New Value.* Palo Alto, CA: Institute of Lesbian Studies, 1988.

Lindsey, Karen. *Friends as Family: New Kinds of Families and What They Could Mean for You.* Boston: Beacon Press, 1981.

Lugones, Maria. "Playfulness, 'World' Travelling, and Loving Perception." In *Lesbian Philosophies and Cultures,* edited by Jeffner Allen. Albany, NY: State Univ. of New York Press, 1990.

Also these films, available on videotape: *Fried Green Tomatoes, Strangers in Good Company, Girlfriends, A Women's Tale.*

Bitches from Hell: The Politics of Self-Defense

Caputi, Jane. *The Age of Sex Crime.* Bowling Green, OH: Bowling Green State Univ. Press, 1987.

Delacost, Frederique, and Felice Newman, eds. *Fight Back: Feminist Resistance to Male Violence.* Minneapolis: Cleis Press, 1981.

Dworkin, Andrea. *Letters from a War Zone: Writings 1976–1989.* New York: E. P. Dutton, 1988.

El Saadawi, Nawal. *Woman at Point Zero.* London: Zed Books, 1975.

Hasselstrom, Linda. "A Peaceful Woman Explains Why She Carries a Gun." *Utne Reader,* May/June 1991.

Miedzian, Myriam. *Boys Will Be Boys: Breaking the Link Between Masculinity and Violence.* New York: Doubleday, 1991.

Morgan, Robin. *The Demon Lover: On the Sexuality of Terrorism.* New York: W. W. Norton, 1989.

Mukherjee, Bharati. *Jasmine.* New York: Fawcett, 1989.

Penelope, Julia. *Speaking Freely: Unlearning the Lies of the Fathers' Tongues.* New York: Pergamon Press, 1990.

Rohrlich, Ruby, and Elaine Baruch, eds. *Women in Search of Utopia: Mavericks and Mythmakers.* New York: Schocken Books, 1984.

Walker, Barbara G. *Amazon.* San Francisco: HarperSanFrancisco, 1992.

Warshaw, Robin. *I Never Called It Rape.* New York: Harper & Row, 1988.

Zahavi, Helen. *The Weekend.* New York: Donald Fine, 1991.

Also these films, available on videotape: *A Question of Silence, Shame,* and *Thelma and Louise.*

The Habit of Freedom: Liberating the Colonized Mind

Adair, Margo. *Working Inside Out: Tools for Change.* Berkeley, CA: Wingbow Press, 1984.

Barry, Kathleen. *Female Sexual Slavery*. New York: Avon Books, 1979.

Bartky, Sandra Lee. *Femininity and Domination: Studies in the Phenomenology of Oppression*. New York: Routledge, 1990.

Butler, Pamela. *Talking to Yourself: Learning the Language of Self-Affirmation*. San Francisco: HarperCollins, 1981, 1991.

Frye, Marilyn. *Willful Virgin: Essays in Feminism 1976–1992*. Freedom, CA: Crossing Press, 1992.

Hagan, Kay Leigh. *Internal Affairs: A Journalkeeping Guidebook for Self-Intimacy*. San Francisco: HarperSanFrancisco, 1990.

———. *Prayers to the Moon: Exercises for Self-Reflection*. San Francisco: HarperSanFrancisco, 1991.

Hawxhurst, Donna, and Sue Morrow. *Living Our Visions: Building Feminist Community*. Tempe, AZ: Fourth World, 1984.

McAllister, Pam. *This River of Courage: Generations of Women's Resistance and Action*. Philadelphia: New Society Publishers, 1991.

Spiegel, Marjorie. *The Dreaded Comparison: Human and Animal Slavery*. New York: Mirror Books, 1989.

Stefan, Verena. *Shedding*. Trans. Johanna Moore and Beth Weckmueller. New York: Daughters Publishing Co., 1978.

Steinem, Gloria. *Revolution from Within: The Book of Self-Esteem*. New York: Little, Brown, 1992.

Walker, Alice. *Possessing the Secret of Joy*. New York: Harcourt Brace Jovanovich, 1992.

Wolf, Naomi. *The Beauty Myth*. New York: Doubleday, 1992.

Woolf, Virginia. *A Room of One's Own*. New York: Harcourt Brace Jovanovich, 1929.

Acknowledgments

My work is blessed by the support of many people. I extend special thanks to the following:

The subscribers to *Fugitive Information* for literally underwriting my work on this book with their interest in a series of unwritten essays, their financial support, their participation in the creative process, their intellectual rigor, their commitment to building feminist community, and their infinite patience;

Deborah Brink, for providing a safe haven for this hotheaded fugitive;

Tom Grady, for his insight and advocacy;

Barbara Moulton, for her deft editing, political vision, and conspiratorial glee;

Terrence Crowley, for his steadfast friendship;

Joanne DeMark, for her wise counsel;

Leslita Williams, for her integrity;

My partners in publishing at Harper San Francisco, especially Lisa Bach, Jo Beaton, Judy Beck, Kevin Bentley, Ani Chimichian, Terri Goff, Matthew Lore, Robin Seaman, and all those fabulous sales representatives.

In addition, I thank these women for providing a precious web of support with their tangible and intangible gifts: Jan Arsenault, River Artz, Maytee Aspuro, Ruth Barrett, Woody Blue, June Bryant, Linda Bryant, Pat Buchanan, Patty Callaghan, Rebecca Clark, Judith Cohen, Norma D'Andrea, Joanne DeMark, Diane Denman, Alix Dobkin, Linda Finnell, Darcy Greder, Mary Jane Hagan, Carol Harrison, Judith Harriss, Pattie Belle Hastings, Marlene Johnson, Cathy Hope, Jennifer Louden, Denise Messina, Cathleen McGuire, Cathy McHenry, Brooks Nelson, Dill O'Hagan, Jona Olsson, Jeanne pasle-green, Carol Plummer, Barbara Price, Deborah Ratliff, Katherine Sadler, Gloria Steinem, Nell Stone, Charlotte Taft, Celeste Tibbets, Lisa Vogl, Lise Weil, and Rita Wuebbeler.

Kay Leigh Hagan travels widely to plot revolution and play cards with other hotheads and heart sisters. She is the author of *Internal Affairs: A Journalkeeping Guidebook for Self-Intimacy* and *Prayers to the Moon: Exercises in Self-Reflection,* and the editor of *Women Respond to the Men's Movement: A Feminist Collection.*